Reclaim the Fire

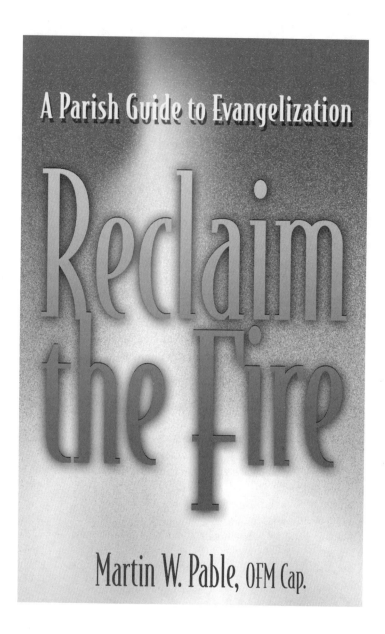

A Parish Guide to Evangelization

Reclaim the Fire

Martin W. Pable, OFM Cap.

ave maria press Notre Dame, Indiana

www.avemariapress.com

International Standard Book Number: 0-87793-963-2

Cover and text design by Kathy Robinson Coleman

Printed and bound in the United States of America.

Library of Congress Cataloging-in-Publication Data
Pable, Martin W.
Reclaim the fire : a parish guide to evangelization / Martin Pable.
     p. cm.
Includes bibliographical references.
ISBN 0-87793-963-2 (pbk.)
1. Evangelistic work--Catholic Church. 2. Church renewal--Catholic
Church. 3. Catholic Church--Membership. I. Title. BX2347.4 .P33 2002
 269'.2'08822--dc21

                     2001007453

                    CIP

Contents

ONE

Where Is the Passion?   7

TWO

A Brief History of Evangelization   23

THREE

A Vision for Evangelization   41

FOUR

What Is "The Good News"?   57

FIVE

Evangelizing Active Catholics   83

SIX

Evangelizing Inactive Catholics and the Unchurched   99

SEVEN

Evangelizing the Culture   125

EIGHT

Becoming an Evangelizing Parish   143

NINE

Evangelization and Apologetics   161

Conclusion   181

Appendix   185

Where Is the Passion?

ONE

A few years ago I wrote an article for an archdiocesan newsletter which I titled "Can the Sleeping Giant Wake Up?" I shared two recent experiences which had jolted me into thinking about the urgency of evangelization. One was an article in *Milwaukee* magazine, a glossy upscale monthly that tells about interesting happenings in and around the city. The article was by a Unitarian minister, George Ezoo, who calls himself "The Church Man" (a take-off, I suppose, on "The Church Lady" of *Saturday Night Live* fame). Ezoo attended weekend services at various churches and temples in the area and wrote his impressions. He also gave a numerical rating to each one. It was fascinating reading.

How did the Catholic churches rate? First, the good news. It was a Catholic parish, Our Lady of Lourdes, that received the highest rating. But there were two pieces of bad news. When Ezoo attended one of the thriving non-denominational megachurches, the pastor told him that 31% of the members are former Catholics. This is consistent with other reports I have seen about the steady loss of our Catholic people to fundamentalist churches. The other disturbing statistic Ezoo quoted was that the number of Catholics in the Archdiocese of

Milwaukee had actually declined between the years 1980 and 1990. Note that these are not just people who still consider themselves Catholic but are simply not practicing their faith; they have stopped calling themselves Catholics. They have abandoned the church. This was the first time I had ever seen clear evidence that the number of Catholics has actually gone down in a given area. It saddened me, and I had no reason to doubt that the same thing has been happening in other dioceses.

The other experience was my attendance at a "ministry leadership seminar" in Michigan sponsored by Promise Keepers. As many readers may know, this is a national movement of Christian men who commit themselves to prayer and spiritual growth, to building strong marriages and families, to put their faith in Christ into daily action, to support their local church and pastor, and to support each other through faith sharing with other men. I had long been involved in directing retreats for men, so I wanted to learn more about this group. I expected to meet thirty to forty pastors at most. What I found was a throng of men—of all ages and occupations—nearly 800 in all. They had given up their Friday night and all day Saturday to come to this conference. The two speakers were positive and inspiring, and each session began with a good half-hour of prayer and song. The enthusiasm of these men was contagious. I don't know if there were any Catholics besides myself in the group, but I found myself thinking: "It's been a long time since I've seen this kind of spiritual energy in our Catholic Church, especially among men."

Urgency for Evangelizing

These two experiences created in me a renewed sense of urgency about evangelizing. I believe we need to ask ourselves some tough questions: Why are we losing so many of our people, especially our youth and our young families? Why are other groups stealing our fire? How can we start reclaiming the gospel vitality that is the very heart of our church?

I was ordained at the end of the 1950s. During our theology studies we would hear about the decline of the church in France, Germany, Holland, Belgium—most of Western Europe. Theologians like Pierre Liege at the University of Paris were calling the church to a rediscovery of the importance of evangelization. After World War II the church tried to maintain "business as usual"—baptizing, confirming, sharing communion, marrying, and ordaining. But the church's ministers, by and large, were out of touch with what was happening culturally. The sacraments and rituals were not touching people where they were living. Preaching, catechesis, and liturgy were not proclaiming the good news of Jesus Christ, not awakening people to conversion and discipleship, not connecting the gospel message with their human longings, joys, anxieties, and sufferings. The church had become a cultural institution with little concern for changing lives toward the vision of Jesus, toward genuine community, or dialogue and critique of the secular culture. And the people were walking away. I remember thinking, "I hope that never happens here."

Disturbing Data

By all appearances, at least, it has not. In April of this year, Catholic News Service reported that the number of people who were received into the church at the Easter Vigil—catechumens and candidates for sacraments—was over 100,000 nationwide. That is a clear index of the continuing appeal of Catholicism to a great many people. But it is not a cause for complacency or triumphalism. For the figure ignores the number of faithful who have left the church. For all we know, the number of "front-door entrants" may have been equaled or surpassed by that of "back-door exits."

It is now twelve years since George Gallup did his famous sociological study on "The Unchurched American." He found that nearly half (44%) of Americans are unchurched; that is, they may believe in God but they either claim no religious affiliation or they do not attend church. Among Catholics, the number of "inactives" was found to be 27%. Remarkably, the criterion for "active" was very broad: If you were baptized Catholic and attended Sunday Mass more than twice a year (excluding Christmas, Easter, weddings, and funerals), you were counted as "active." By that minimal definition, 27% of baptized Catholics are no longer practicing their faith, though many still identify themselves as Catholics. I always say: If a business or company was losing more than one-fourth of its customers, it would not ignore the data. It would call for an analysis and create some action strategies. More recently, Wade Clark Roof's study (*A Generation of Seekers*, 1993) found that only 50% of Catholic baby boomers are currently active in the Catholic Church today; another 8% are active in other churches, and the rest have simply dropped out.

My point is: Many thoughtful people are coming to realize that we cannot simply keep doing things as we've always done them. It is not working. Apart from the priest shortage, another reality is confronting us: we are no longer a growing church. We are a declining church and a graying church. Some years ago George Gallup (an Episcopalian) used the image of "a sleeping giant" to describe the Catholic Church. He was trying to say: You Catholics have so much potential for good in this society. You have the largest membership of any church in America (some sixty million). You have clear teachings, a rich spirituality, visible organization and leadership. But you are asleep. You are not having the spiritual impact on the society that you could have—and the nation is poorer for it.

Part of the problem, I believe, is that we Catholics have become entangled in our own internal squabbles. These are consuming the energy and vitality that could be turned outward for mission and impact on our world. The figures cited above can be seized upon by both liberals and conservatives to further their own agendas. Liberals can say: "Of course—people are leaving the church and refusing to connect because of undemocratic structures of authority, outmoded teachings on sexual issues, insistence on mandatory celibacy for priests, and refusal to include women in priestly and leadership roles. What is needed is obvious: a new agenda that will bring about meaningful reform." And from their corner, the conservatives can reply: "The real problem is—the American church has sold out to the spirit of relativism and individualism in the culture. Who would want to join a church that is so riddled with controversy and allows everyone to pick and choose their own beliefs and moral choices? What is needed is obvious: a return to traditional teachings, forms of worship, and structures of authority."

There may be some truth in both these positions. But this is not a time for blaming. Some of us remember the 1950s debates over "Who lost China to the Communists?" Similar debates over "Who's driving people away from the church?" would be a total waste of time and energy. Certainly, the grand vision of Vatican II must continue to unfold and become enfleshed in our church's life. This is not a time for stagnation or retrenching. But the church will never be all that it should be. If we wait for it to become perfect before we begin evangelizing, we will never begin. Too often our parishes remain stuck in a "maintenance" mentality. Parish life is seen as maintaining the buildings and programs that served people's needs in the past. Important questions do not get asked: "Have the needs changed—so that we have to devise new programs and ministries to meet them?" And just as urgent:

❧ Are we totally preoccupied with "saving the saved," taking care of our own—but ignoring those many people who are not gathering with us?

❧ Are we making any efforts to reach out to the inactive Catholics and unchurched people in our midst?

❧ Are we even thinking of those many people who are searching for something to believe in and hope for, but are reluctant to make the first move to seek us out?

In a word: Are we trying to move from a maintenance parish to an evangelizing, mission-driven parish?

At the Center: Jesus Christ

I want to be perfectly clear on this next point: The purpose of the church is not to increase its membership rolls. The purpose of the church is to make known the person and the message of Jesus Christ. The church is not the center; Jesus is. I will never forget what I once heard Bishop Raymond Lucker say: "Too many Catholics have been catechized and sacramentalized—but never evangelized. They have never formed a personal relationship with Jesus Christ. And I don't blame them. We taught them for years that you become a Catholic by learning a set of truths and obeying a set of rules. But we never taught them *to know the Lord.*"

If this is true—and I believe it is—would it not explain what we said above about the defection of so many Catholics in post-war Western Europe? Would it not help us understand the disaffection of many American Catholics today? Doctrines, sacraments, rituals—wonderful and necessary as they are—will not of themselves capture the human heart or nourish its spiritual hungers. It is the personal relationship with Jesus Christ that gives doctrines, sacraments, and rituals their meaning. How else can we understand the following anecdote? Some good Catholic parents once told me that their young adult son had joined an evangelical church. When they asked him why, he replied, in all sincerity, "I had to leave the Catholic Church in order to find Jesus Christ." How sad. Even if he is being dramatic and self-justifying, doesn't the question have to be asked: "How do we go off track like this? How can we insure that Jesus will always be the center of our teaching, preaching, and worship?" If Jesus is not a real person for us, if his life and teachings do not thrill us with joy, people will always find our religion disappointing.

Insights From the New Testament

With that in mind, I would like to make a brief excursion into the New Testament. How did the early church understand its mission to proclaim the good news of Jesus? Luke's gospel portrays Jesus himself as the original "good news" (Lk 4:14-21). He came to Galilee, Luke says, "in the power of the Spirit," just as earlier he was "filled with the holy Spirit" and "was led by the Spirit into the desert" to be tempted by Satan (Lk 4:1). He came to his home town of Nazareth and entered the synagogue on the Sabbath "according to his custom" (vs. 16); or, as another translation reads, "as he was in the habit of doing." I like to reference that phrase when people ask why they should bother attending church on Sunday: "I can pray better at home or out in the woods," they say. To which I reply: "Well, we know Jesus prayed alone too, but he also made sure he joined the community for worship together. He needed to hear the Hebrew scriptures proclaimed and interpreted, he needed to praise God in prayer and song with his people. If anyone could have separated himself from communal worship, it would have been Jesus; yet he chose not to. Isn't there an important lesson there for all of us?"

But on with the story. "He stood up to read and was handed a scroll of the prophet Isaiah. He unrolled the scroll and found the passage [i.e., he knew what he was looking for] where it was written:

> The Spirit of the Lord is upon me,
> because he has anointed me
> to bring glad tidings ["good news"]
> to the poor.
>
> He has sent me to proclaim liberty to captives. . .
> to let the oppressed go free,
> and to proclaim a year acceptable to the Lord"
> (vv. 17-19).

Every devout Jew was familiar with that passage. It gave them hope, during their years of exile in Babylon, that God would some day restore them to their homeland. But how were they to understand this passage in their own time, when their homeland itself was under domination by the Roman powers? Would Jesus promise to lead them to a victorious overthrow of their oppressors? It was a dramatic moment. "The eyes of all in the synagogue looked intently at him," the text says, waiting for his next words. "He said to them, 'Today this scripture passage is fulfilled in your hearing'" (vv. 20-21). A murmur of excitement rippled through the crowd. Could this be the Messiah? Will he call us to unite behind him, be ready to take up arms for our freedom?

But soon disappointment set in. Luke does not give us Jesus' words, but we can infer the main content of his message from the rest of the gospel. What Jesus held up for his listeners was a spiritual vision and fulfillment of Isaiah's prophecy. The "glad tidings" are: I have been sent by God to assure you that he has not abandoned you. Even in your oppression, you remain God's beloved sons and daughters. Nothing can take that away from you. If you believe in me and my words, you will be inwardly free, no matter your external condition. You will be spiritually rich, no matter your material poverty.

But his message was resisted. It was not what they wanted to hear. Disappointment turned to hostility as they dismissed him as no more than one of their own. Who does he think he is, claiming he is "sent by God?" Just another deluded paranoiac, puffed up with his own self-importance. Finally, hostility turned to violence: "They rose up, drove him out of the town, and led him to the brow of the hill on which their town had been built, to hurl him down headlong. But he passed through the midst of them and went away" (vv. 29-30).

A lesser man would have withdrawn from the public eye at this point and settled for a more conventional way of life. But the gospels show Jesus continuing his mission. His teachings affirmed the worth and dignity of every person, even as they challenged the complacency of the political and religious elites. His miracles, particularly his healings, revealed the compassion of God for his suffering children. His promise of eternal life for God's faithful ones gave hope to those who saw the unjust prosper at the expense of the just. And he assured the unjust that they would have no part in God's kingdom unless they reformed their ways.

Sent to Evangelize

Besides teaching and healing, Jesus was spending much of his time forming his chosen disciples for the continuation of his mission. When he felt they were ready, he sent them out. I picture that initial sending as sort of a "trial run" or "getting their feet wet." Matthew describes the scene this way: Jesus had been passing through the towns and villages of Galilee, "proclaiming the gospel of the kingdom [of God] and curing every disease and illness. At the sight of the crowds, his heart was moved with pity for them because they were troubled and abandoned, like sheep without a shepherd" (Mt 9:35-36). The Old Testament prophets, particularly Jeremiah and Ezekiel, had also pictured God's people as sheep who were "scattered" or "wandering aimlessly." The image is that of people who are spiritually hungry and desolate. What did Jesus do? Two things. First, he asked the disciples to pray that God may send "laborers" (evangelists) to help them. And second, he empowered the disciples themselves to bring the good news of the gospel to those who are spiritually exhausted (Mt 9:37–10:7).

But the definitive "sending" took place at the ascension, the last words of Jesus recorded in the gospels. According to Matthew, Jesus gathered the disciples together and addressed them in solemn words: "All power in heaven and on earth has been given to me. Go, therefore, and make disciples of all nations, baptizing them in the name of the Father, and of the Son, and of the holy Spirit, teaching them to observe all that I have commanded you. And behold, I am with you always, until the end of the age" (Mt 28:18b-20). The words are similar in the gospels of Mark (16:15-16) and Luke (24:46-49). This scene is often called "the great commissioning." Jesus makes it clear that the church does not exist for its own sake. It has a mission, a purpose. It must not let the world forget Jesus Christ. It must continue to make him known and to proclaim his teachings everywhere in the world until time is no more.

The Acts of the Apostles is the story of how the first disciples carried out the mission entrusted to them. Transformed by the outpouring of the Holy Spirit at Pentecost, Peter and the others spoke powerfully to the assembled crowd. You all remember, they said, how Jesus of Nazareth went about doing good among the people and healing them of their afflictions. Yet he was condemned unjustly by the authorities and handed over to be crucified. But—incredible as it seems—God raised him from the dead and made him Lord and Savior of the whole human family. The apostles spoke with such conviction that those who listened "were cut to the heart, and they asked Peter and the other apostles, 'What are we to do, my brothers?' Peter said to them, 'Repent and be baptized, every one of you, in the name of Jesus Christ for the forgiveness of your sins; and you will receive the gift of the holy Spirit'" (Acts 2:37-38). In other words: Turn away from sin, commit yourself to Jesus Christ and his way of life, and receive baptism as the sign of rebirth into the new family of God. "Those who accepted his message were baptized, and about three thousand persons were added that day" (Acts 2:41).

"Added" to what? To the community of believers, later to be called "the church." This was an important piece. Believers in Jesus were not a group of independent individuals. They were connected to a visible community of people who "devoted themselves to the teaching of the apostles and to the communal life, to the breaking of the bread and to the prayers" (Acts 2:42). They formed a community committed to growing in their knowledge of Christ and his teachings, to communal prayer and worship, and to caring for one another—to the point that "there was no needy person among them" (4:34). Non-believers were struck by the joy and love rippling through this new community, with the result that "great favor was accorded them all" (4:33) and "every day the Lord added to their number those who were being saved" (2:47).

It is clear that the first Christians were converts from Judaism and that they saw themselves as a sect within Judaism. As time went on, however, they separated more and more from the Jewish mainstream and began to think of themselves as a new religion, but in historical and theological continuity with Judaism. One of the most dramatic developments in the early church's awareness of its mission was the decision to extend the proclamation of the gospel and invitation to discipleship to people of Gentile origin. First, Peter had his famous vision whereby he understood that no person should be in principle excluded from the Christian community. This development is fully described in chapter 10 of the Acts of the Apostles. Not long after, some in the community reasoned that not only should Gentiles be welcomed, they should be told the story of Jesus and actively invited to faith and baptism (Acts 11:19ff.). Next, the Holy Spirit inspired the community at Antioch in Syria to send Barnabas and Paul on a mission to spread the gospel of Jesus to both Jews and Gentiles beyond the borders of Palestine. Thus the church became, consciously, a missionary, evangelizing community.

An interesting question: What was the process whereby new members connected with the community? My own speculation goes something like this. The first Christian converts from Judaism lived their newfound faith, not in an ostentatious way, but in a way that was convincing. Their Jewish and Gentile neighbors observed how the Christians were devoted to their families, were conscientious in their jobs, did not go along with the immoral sexual practices of the time, and reached out in care to those who were poor or sick. Moreover, they did all this with a spirit of joy and peacefulness. At some point the Jew or Gentile would say, "You know, you've changed. What's happened to you?" And the new Christian would say, "You're right—I've come to know Jesus Christ, and it's made all the difference." "Well, tell me about him." And the Christian would tell the story of Jesus. If the other person was ready (and touched by divine grace) he or she would say, "That's what I'm looking for. What do I need to do?" The Christian would then introduce the person to the community and (later) to the catechumenate. I just don't think there were many "mass conversions" after Pentecost. Rather, most people found their way into the church through the authentic witness and one-on-one connections with believing Christians.

Early Evangelizers

I like to think of the woman of Samaria (Jn 4:1-42) as the first lay evangelist. After being both accepted by Jesus for who she was and challenged by him for her lifestyle, she ran to tell the townsfolk about him: "Come and see a man who told me everything I have done. Could he possibly be the Messiah?" (Jn 4:29). One suspects she would not be considered the most credible person in town. Yet her earnest and dignified manner convinced a good number of Samaritans to come and see for themselves (vs. 39). After meeting with Jesus they did the unthinkable: they invited this Jew, with whom they would ordinarily never associate, to stay with them for a few days. Some, at least, became convinced of what the woman was daring to claim. They said to her, "We no longer believe because of your word; for we have heard for ourselves, and we know that this is truly the savior of the world" (Jn 4:42). We don't know how deep or lasting these "conversions" were. But the story is meant to reveal the spiritual impact one person can have through the force of his or her testimony. Interestingly, the Acts of the Apostles tells how a disciple named Philip, some time after the Pentecost event, went to Samaria and began speaking about Jesus as the crucified and risen Messiah. Once again the Samaritans were receptive, especially when his preaching was accompanied by healings and expulsion of demons. The result: "There was great joy in that city" (Acts 8:8).

Philip is not named as one of the twelve apostles, so he may well have been another lay evangelist. We find him next on the road from Jerusalem toward the Gaza desert (Acts 8:26-40). The Holy Spirit directed him to catch up with an Ethiopian man riding in a chariot. The man appears to be a "minority" person on at least two counts: He is (most likely) black-skinned, and the fact that he is described as "a eunuch" indicates that he suffers from some kind of sexual dysfunction. Whether the cause was physical or psychological, the man is sexually impotent. It is not hard to imagine him as the butt of jokes and put-downs in his cultural environment. Being in charge of the queen's treasury, he is probably quite a wealthy man. However, he is also a lonely man.

But spiritually he is a seeker. He "had come on a pilgrimage to Jerusalem," the text says. He may have been a convert to Judaism, but more likely he was a Gentile "God-fearer"—one who accepted Jewish monotheism and morality, but did not become a full convert. He was obviously searching for something more, something to help him find meaning in his life. He makes a religious pilgrimage. He is reading the Jewish scriptures. He asks Philip to help him understand the passage from Isaiah about "the suffering servant." Philip uses the text as a springboard to tell him the good news of Jesus. The Ethiopian is deeply touched by the grace of God and asks Philip for baptism. So here again we have that remarkable combination: one person who is searching for God's truth and love, and another who is filled with enthusiasm for sharing that very message with others.

Let us consider one final example of lay evangelizers in the New Testament. We read in Acts 18 about a married couple, Priscilla and Aquila, who were banished from Rome, along with other Jews, by the emperor Claudius. They came to Corinth, where they met Paul and became Christians. Later they moved to Ephesus, where they instructed a Jewish man named Apollos who had come to believe that Jesus was the fulfillment of the Old Testament promises. But he had not been fully catechized or baptized into the Christian community. So Priscilla and Aquila completed the initiation process with him. The community recognized his remarkable gifts of biblical knowledge and eloquent speech, sending him on to Greece to continue his evangelizing ministry. Paul held Priscilla and Aquila in high regard. In one letter he publicly thanks them because they "risked their necks for my life" (Rom 16:4), and in several others he sends special greetings to them and to "the church" that meets at their house (1 Cor 16:19; 2 Tm 4:19).

It is evident, then, that the early church understood itself as called by Christ and empowered by the Holy Spirit to bring the good news of Jesus to all peoples in all parts of the known world. Clearly also, this was seen as the mission of the entire church community, not just the apostles, "elders," and other authority figures. Every Christian, by virtue of his or her baptism, was to make Christ and his saving message known and loved. Christians were to do so first of all by the quality of their lives, their good example, their "wordless witness," to use a later expression of Pope Paul VI. But secondly, they were to witness to Christ also by their words, their verbal testimony. They were not to hesitate to speak to others about what they believed and why they chose to live as they did. The First Letter of Peter takes this evangelizing activity for granted when he reminds his readers: "Always be ready to give an explanation to anyone who asks you for a reason for your hope" (1 Pt 3:15). The assumption was: Jews and Gentiles would sometimes be curious about what Christians believed and why; so Christians ought to be able to speak about this with joy and conviction. But they are to avoid any kind of arrogance or coercion, for the letter adds, "but do it with gentleness and reverence" (vs. 16).

And so the Christian gospel spread, even amid harassment and persecution. The church of the early Christian centuries was unmistakably an evangelizing community, proclaiming belief in its Lord and Savior with fervent passion. We turn now to look at what happened to that energy in the centuries that followed.

A Brief
History of
Evangelization

The previous chapter was titled "Where Is the Passion?" We saw that the Catholic Church today, at least in the United States and much of Western Europe, appears to be in a state of apathy in regard to evangelization. We recall how George Gallup used the image of "a sleeping giant" to characterize the church at the present moment. By contrast, we saw that the early church had a deep passion for spreading the gospel of Jesus Christ to all parts of the world. What has happened in the intervening centuries?

This brief excursion into history will necessarily be superficial, my purpose being to provide some understanding of how we may have lost the evangelizing energy of the past. I am indebted to David Bohr for the material that follows. A fuller treatment may be found in his fine volume *Evangelization in America* (Paulist Press, 1977).

Post-Apostolic Era

From the very beginning Christians experienced opposition and persecution, first from mainstream Judaism and later from the Roman government. The periods of persecution were interspersed with times of peace, at least in many regions of the Empire. At any rate, during these first centuries after Christ, we have no record of formal missionary endeavors on the part of the Christian church. The Christians embodied their faith in daily action and celebrated it in the liturgy. While being evangelized themselves through proclamation of God's Word and participation in the sacraments, they evangelized their unbelieving neighbors mainly by the witness of their lives and their readiness to share their faith in the Lord Jesus. Moreover, the willingness of so many to endure confiscation of their possessions, imprisonment, and even martyrdom for their faith inspired unbelievers to join their ranks. One other form of evangelization was the effort of the so-called "Apologists"—Justin Martyr, Irenaeus, Origen, Tertullian—to explain and defend Christian beliefs and practices to non-Christian critics. The cumulative result of these low-key forms of evangelizing was remarkable. According to Bohr, by the start of the fourth century there were an estimated seven million Christians in a total population of fifty million in the Roman Empire. And geographically, the church had spread to Gaul, Spain, and the marginal zones of Germany and Britain in the West and as far as Edessa in the East.

Then, with the conversion of the Emperor Constantine and the Edict of Milan in 313, the persecution of the Christians ceased. Later, in 380, the imperial decree of Theodosius the Great made Christianity the official religion of the Roman Empire. Now, ironically, all citizens were required to become Christians under pain of legal sanctions. As Bohr says, "A new volume in Church history and in the evangelization process was being prepared" (p. 56). For one thing, as Christianity became more and more identified with the Empire, it tended to become fashionable. Also, baptism was no longer a life-changing decision following a rigorous period of discernment and preparation; it was "the thing to do" in order to be accepted into the dominant culture. This meant that many professing Christians were no longer interested in living the radical demands of the gospel. Christianity could become a soft and comfortable form of religion. As a result, those Christians who desired a more vigorous and radical following of Christ chose the monastic or eremitical form of life as a way of separating themselves from the culture.

Another result, according to Bohr, was that a new principle of evangelization evolved. In the early church, people were first evangelized (by the example and verbal witness of believing Christians); next they were catechized—through a lengthy process of instruction in the scriptures, the life and teachings of Jesus, the Christian mysteries—and only then were they baptized and admitted to full communion with the church. Now, however, the process was reversed: Christians were baptized first (often as infants or children), and only then were they catechized and evangelized. Moreover, these latter two processes were often truncated. As Bohr says:

> As the organization of the Empire waned, the Church admitted to her fold new populations who had no education nor culture of their own. Amid ignorance, pagan customs and different languages, the new converts were in no sense familiar with the Gospel. . . . The missionaries sent out to these new peoples could hope for little more than having them learn by rote the Our Father and the Creed. A spiritual life based on Scripture was rapidly replaced with more popular forms of religious piety based on the cult of local saints, miracles and relics. Participation in liturgical and sacramental acts was reduced to a mere matter of obligation (pp. 56-57).

Gradually, through periods of controversies, heresies, and moral laxity, evangelization was replaced by catechesis and ritual: "what I must believe and do in order to be saved," rather than "what God has done for us in Christ Jesus." The result was a large number of poorly instructed "cultural" or "sociological" Catholics who were Christian in name only. The stage was set for the breakaway evangelical sects of the Middle Ages and the eventual large-scale Protestant Reformation. Meanwhile, the discoveries of new lands and peoples in the fifteenth and sixteenth centuries opened a whole new period of missionary activity. However, the process of evangelization often became identified solely with the conversion and baptism of "pagan" peoples. It remained for the Second Vatican Council to formulate a more theologically adequate vision of mission.

The Immigrant Church in the United States

We turn now to a brief look at the history of evangelization in the United States. I will base this material mainly on William Portier's article on "Catholic Evangelization in the United States" (Kenneth Boyack, ed., *The New Catholic Evangelization*, Paulist Press, 1992, pp. 27-41). Beginning with the early republic, Portier says, it is difficult to imagine how tiny the Catholic community was in the year 1776. Less than one percent of the population was Catholic, found mostly in Maryland and Pennsylvania. There were fewer than thirty priests for the whole country. The first bishop, John Carroll, was appointed in 1789. For many years penal laws forbade Catholics to worship in public; so the family became "the domestic church" and priests served as "circuit riders" bringing religious instruction and the sacraments to small groups of Catholics gathered in homes.

As the colonies (and later the states) became more religiously tolerant in the nineteenth century, waves of immigrant Catholics began to cross the ocean from Europe. Amazingly, by the middle of the century

Catholics had become the largest single denomination in the country. The great fear among their families and relatives back in Europe was that the immigrants would lose their Catholic faith in a land thought to be populated by "pagans and heretics." So the primary focus of the immigrants was to preserve their faith—what Portier calls "internal evangelization." It is not difficult to imagine the process. As soon as a group of Catholics settled in a city neighborhood or rural community, they pooled their resources, often at great sacrifice, to build a church and recruit a priest to be their pastor. If they were prosperous enough, they would then build a school and seek nuns to staff it so they would be able to pass on their faith to the next generation.

Because they received no support from the government, these Catholics had to work hard and collaboratively in order to build and maintain these structures. Fortunately, they often received a great deal of financial help from the mission aid societies in Europe. Another force that bound immigrant Catholics together was the fact that (at least in the cities) the parish became a "total environment" providing many forms of material, spiritual, and emotional support. Extended families and close neighborhoods, as well as a common language and ethnic customs bonded people together. Besides Sunday Mass, the parish church offered opportunities for devotions, processions, parish missions ("revivals"), and the mythic figure of the pastor who would listen, comfort, challenge, and dispense the church's wisdom and sacraments. The nuns in the school provided religious instruction as well as a solid education and discipline for generations of children. Catholic hospitals and orphanages, as well as the St. Vincent de Paul Society, were available to care for people in times of need. The parish even became the center of recreation: picnics, festivals, concerts, dances, softball and bowling teams, and the like.

The immigrant parish, then, was a safe harbor wherein immigrant Catholics could find identity as well as nourishment and support for their faith. On the other hand, it lacked a sense of mission, of outreach beyond "our own." The parish had all it could do to serve the spiritual and social needs of the immigrants who continued to pour into the urban or rural areas. "Maintenance" rather than "mission" was the priority. This direction was further reinforced by the experience of discrimination that many immigrant Catholics had to endure. Outside their own enclaves, Catholics often felt a sense of hostility, ridicule, and outright rejection by mainstream society. So they had no inclination to try to share their faith or explain their beliefs to "outsiders." As time went on and their desire for acceptance and assimilation into the dominant culture grew, Catholics became increasingly "bashful" about talking with others about their faith. The very word "evangelization" disappeared from their vocabulary. They were encouraged to pray and give good example so that others might become "converts" to the faith, especially their non-Catholic spouses or friends. But by and large they kept the faith to themselves.

However, Portier reminds us, there were some notable exceptions. One was the so-called "Negro Missions." After the Civil War, the second and third plenary Councils of Baltimore called for the evangelization of freed slaves. One of the pioneers in this endeavor was Josephite Fr. John Slattery. He urged his religious community to reach out to African-Americans with the message of Catholicism and even advocated a black Catholic clergy during the days of segregated seminaries. But his efforts to integrate the seminaries were rebuffed and he became embittered by the racism he found in the church. Eventually he left the church, but the Josephites have continued their mission to African-Americans to the present day.

Another notable effort at outreach was the "Indian Missions." Most evangelization of Native Americans took place through the establishment of mission schools, mainly through the Jesuits in the East and the Franciscans in the West. The recently canonized Mother Katherine Drexel was perhaps the most influential advocate of evangelization among Native Americans. Born in Philadelphia, she was the daughter of a wealthy banker. She was first introduced to the Indian Missions in the early 1880s. After her father died, she devoted her life and her considerable inheritance to the missions, eventually founding "the Sisters of the Blessed Sacrament for Indians and Colored People." During the twentieth century, millions of dollars of Drexel money financed mission schools and churches throughout the South and West.

Another strong figure in Catholic evangelization during the immigrant years was Isaac Hecker. He was born into a Jewish family but became a convert to Catholicism in the mid-1800s. He became convinced that the truths of the faith would have an appeal to every fair-minded person. He saw the religious freedom in America—and even church-state separation—as a providential opportunity to evangelize the nation by persuasion. His dream was to present the truths of Catholicism in such an appealing way that people would embrace the faith freely. In this way he hoped to transform the whole culture and bring about unity amid so much diversity. In one of his writings he made the bold claim that "The Catholic Church alone is able to give unity to a people, composed of such conflicting elements as ours, and to form them into a great nation" (quoted in Portier, p. 32). Hecker was passionately American as well as Catholic. He went on to be ordained a priest and later founded the Missionary Society of St. Paul the Apostle, popularly known as "the Paulists." They have maintained their founder's charism through the years and today are recognized as leaders in evangelization.

One who inherited Father Hecker's dream of the conversion of America was his Paulist disciple, Walter Elliott. After publishing a biography of Hecker, Elliott devoted himself full time to speaking to non-Catholics about Catholicism. First in small towns, later in cities like Detroit and Cleveland, Elliott gathered people in town halls. He spoke without clerical collar and used a simple format: a hymn, a question box, then a presentation. His style was gentle and persuasive, trying to present the truths of Catholicism as the fulfillment of people's deepest human needs and longings. Later he developed a one-year study program to train priests to conduct these "missions" to non-Catholics. They had some success. In the first thirteen years of the missions in the diocese of Cleveland, there were some 1600 converts. But these numbers were not sufficient to gather continued support for Elliott's approach. A few years after 1900, the missions to non-Catholics effectively ended.

Consolidation: 1908-Vatican II

By 1908 the Catholic Church in the United States was abundantly blessed with its own structures of parishes, schools, charitable institutions, seminaries, and hierarchy. Accordingly, the Vatican declared that it was no longer "a mission" but a fully established church. Though the Paulist dream of converting Protestant America had faded, evangelization efforts continued. A country pastor from the Detroit archdiocese, Fr. Francis Kelley, put forth a view of urban America as corrupt and godless. The hope for the church, he claimed, was in rural America. In his travels he was shocked to find many rural Catholics without churches and pastors; their faith was in danger of being lost. His response was to found The Church Extension

Society out of Chicago. A great fund raiser, he collected money to build chapels and schools in the South, West, and Appalachia. He caught the imagination of many Catholics by making use of special railroad "chapel cars," named after different saints, whereby priests and lay missionaries rode into rural towns and valleys to strengthen the faith of Catholics and evangelize any unbelievers who would listen. According to Portier, "No single person did more than Kelley to raise Catholic evangelization consciousness in the early twentieth century" (p. 34).

Perhaps nothing signaled the coming of age of the church in the United States more than the founding of its first foreign mission society. Not only was the American church no longer a mission territory—it was sending American-formed missionaries into foreign lands. In 1911, Fathers James Walsh and Thomas Price founded "The Catholic Foreign Mission Society of America," better known as "Maryknoll." In 1918, the Society sent its first missionaries to China. Soon it began publishing its own magazine, *Field Afar*, which later was changed to *Maryknoll*. The small magazine, complete with photos, brought the foreign missions into countless Catholic homes. It was not long before most religious orders headquartered in this country were sending missionaries to foreign lands. During most of the twentieth century, American Catholics supported the missions generously with both money and vocations. Missionaries home on vacation would speak to school children and parish groups, while women's auxiliaries made vestments and altar linens for the missions.

Moreover, Catholic laity began to get involved in evangelism. When anti-Catholicism surfaced in the defeat of Alfred Smith, a Catholic running for president in 1928, a group of lay Catholics founded The Catholic Information Society. Their purpose was to present the teachings of the faith in a clear and persuasive manner, using books, pamphlets, and inquiry classes. A bold form of evangelism that began in England came to this country in 1931 in the form of The Catholic Evidence Guild. The group trained lay men and women as "street preachers" who would speak to open-air groups in parks, on street corners, or wherever crowds could gather. By 1935, branches of the Guild had sprung up in major cities such as New York, Baltimore, Washington, Philadelphia, and Oklahoma City. Members were trained not only in giving clear and appealing presentations, but also in dealing with questions and hecklers from the audience. A branch at Rosary College in Illinois would send students as "women missionaries" into the rural towns of Oklahoma, Louisiana, and North Carolina during the summer months. They billed themselves as "street preachers" who offered "revivals" from the back of pickup trucks. They would make use of lively music as well as question-and-answer exchanges. The Evidence Guild is still active today, at least in New York City.

In 1936, William Howard Bishop, a diocesan priest in rural Maryland, wrote an article in a clergy magazine in which he put forth a plan to evangelize rural America, somewhat in the spirit of Fr. Francis Kelley three decades earlier. In 1939 he was invited by the archbishop of Cincinnati to put his plan into action. Bishop formed The Home Missioners of America, known more popularly as "Glenmary." The missioners, in collaboration with lay members, specialized in open-air and tent preaching in remote rural areas. Their aim was not only to make converts but also to help improve the material and spiritual lives of the people, whether or not they accepted the faith.

Finally, it should be noted that while few lay Catholics saw themselves as preachers, a significant number wanted to do more to share their faith than pray and contribute to the missions. The movement known as "Catholic Action," brought to this country from Europe after World War II, gave Catholic laity motivation and skills to evangelize by living and speaking about their faith in the midst of the secular world. Under the name of Young Christian Workers, Young Christian Students, and the Christian Family Movement, these groups did not so much attempt to make converts as to deepen their own faith and work to transform their environment with gospel values.

Vatican II and Its Aftermath

The Second Vatican Council (1962-65) had very little focus on evangelization. The church at that time was preoccupied with its own self-understanding and need for internal renewal. As has been observed, this was the first time in history that an ecumenical council dealt explicitly with the question: "What is the Church—and its mission?" There were, however, a couple of references to evangelization. One was in *Lumen Gentium*, the document on the nature of the church, where it was clearly stated that every baptized disciple of Christ (not just bishops and priests) *has the obligation of spreading the faith* to the best of his or her ability (n. 17). This powerful notion is not developed any further, however. The other reference is in the decree on the church's missionary activity (*Ad Gentes*). The document speaks of the value of Christian *witness* in proclaiming the gospel. It states that "witness" includes not only giving good example and speaking about one's faith in Christ, but also being involved in building a better society according to God's plan. This would include, for example, such secular activities as improving education, overcoming hunger and disease, providing decent housing, and working for better government. Thus "human development" is seen as a genuine form of missionary activity—and, by extension, of evangelization.

Decline of Evangelization

At this point I would like to make a claim with which some readers may disagree. In my opinion, after Vatican II the evangelizing dimension of the gospel was largely lost in this country. By no means am I "blaming" the Council for this loss. I believe there were a number of understandable reasons why evangelization got lost:

1. Parishes became preoccupied with internal issues. They were required to adapt the liturgical reforms envisioned by the Council. They had to improve parochial schools in order to keep them competitive with public schools. They had to bring their catechetical materials and methods up to date; this was especially true in the areas of morality, which were being seriously challenged by the secular society. And they had to initiate new forms of lay participation such as parish councils and committees. All this involved tremendous investments of time and energy. There simply was none left for mission or evangelization.

2. The church in this country got involved in the pressing social issues of the time: racism and integration; poverty; hunger; health care; the Vietnam War; nuclear weapons. We simply could not stand by without raising our voices and directing our resources in the service of these great concerns.

3. Many Catholics were moving out of their immigrant parishes into "mainstream" America. The immigrant parish had served them well. They learned to speak English, they received a quality education, they were able to attend prestigious colleges and universities. Now they desired full acceptance into the professional and corporate world. "Evangelization" or "Christian witness"

were far from their minds. They were hesitant even to acknowledge their Catholicism, much less to share it with their peers. Moreover, they had come to accept the American value of pluralism: "live and let live." The popular slogan goes: "There are two things you don't talk about: politics and religion." In addition, many Catholics grew up without a clear knowledge of their beliefs, so they felt inadequate to explain or defend them if challenged.

4. One final factor behind the slippage in evangelization: "Making converts" was perceived as both socially ungracious and theologically unacceptable. Questions like these became commonplace: "Why should we try to impose our beliefs on anyone else?" "What makes us think our particular religion is better than anyone else's?" These attitudes were strongly reinforced when Catholics encountered groups of Christian fundamentalists and Jehovah's Witnesses trying to convince them of the errors of their Catholic beliefs. These experiences, plus the scandals of some of the televangelists, gave evangelization a negative image in the minds of many Catholics.

The overall result: Catholics, as a group, became bashful about their faith. Portier's closing remarks express it very well:

The greatest obstacle to Catholics becoming more evangelical is their general acceptance of American religious pluralism as a kind of ideal natural state in which people are best left alone with their beliefs. This secular-pluralist approach to church-state separation dates to the beginning of our century and ignores the need for public discussion about the deepest shared basis for this culture. In such a view, imagining effective ways to share faith life with inactive Catholics or the unchurched appears as somehow in poor taste, an impolite invasion of privacy or even un-American. Catholics who are really serious about evangelization as transformation of culture from within must learn to behave more as fired-up evangelicals than as civil republicans or pugnacious immigrants (p. 39).

Rebirth of Evangelization

Meanwhile, Pope Paul VI saw what was happening: the church was becoming inward-looking and self-preoccupied. It was losing its outward, missionary, evangelizing energy. He was moved to call, in 1974, the third worldwide Synod of Bishops and to focus the agenda on evangelization. By way of preparation, he asked all the bishops to reflect ahead of time on what he called "three burning questions," which I paraphrase as follows:

1. "In our time, what has happened to the hidden energy of the gospel?" In other words: Why are we so bogged down in internal squabbles and controversies, while the power of the gospel to transform human lives remains trapped?

2. "Is the gospel of Christ still relevant to the people of modern times—or must it give way to some other ideology?" (In the latter case, of course, there would be no point in meeting—except to talk to ourselves).

3. "If you believe the gospel is still relevant, then what methods should be used to proclaim it more effectively?"

The pope realized these would be provocative, even dangerous, questions. But he wanted to highlight the seriousness of the situation and have the bishops come well prepared to deal with it. When the Synod assembled, the bishops shared the experiences and struggles of their local churches around the world and proposed various solutions. They agreed that a new evangelization was needed, but were unable to agree on a written document. So they asked the pope to write it, based on their reflections. The result was what has been called "The Magna Carta" of evangelization: the apostolic exhortation of Pope Paul VI *On Evangelization in the Modern World* (Dec. 8, 1975). The document attracted very little notice at the time, being overshadowed in the media by the Vatican's "Declaration on Sexual Ethics" that came out about a month later. To this day I have not found many people who have read Pope Paul's document (or even heard of it). I myself did not see it until two years later. But reading it was life-changing for me. Unlike most papal documents (which I find ponderous and laborious), this one has fire, passion, and clarity. Here are just a few of the highlights:

🖊 Evangelization is not just a response to a present crisis; it is the church's *normal* activity.

🖊 In fact, evangelization is the church's *primary and essential mission.* Therefore, it is not an "optional" activity—something we can get around to some day when we have everything else in place in our parishes. It ought to take central place, top priority.

🖊 Every person in the world has a right to at least *hear* about Jesus Christ and his gospel. They are free to accept or reject it, but the church *must* proclaim it. (This point was made in opposition to those who were saying that the church should stop its missionary activity; or at most, be involved in helping indigenous people improve their living conditions and be faithful to their own religious beliefs).

🖊 Therefore, every baptized Catholic has the corresponding *duty* to make known the person and message of Jesus in whatever ways they can—by the witness of their example, by their willingness to speak of what they believe, and by working together with others to build a more just and human society.

❧ In evangelizing, the church must never try to impose the gospel upon people by force or by manipulation. Rather, we should help people to recognize the presence and action of God already present in their lives and culture, show them how belief in Christ can further transform them, then trust in the grace of the Holy Spirit to lead them to a free decision.

Unfortunately, the pope's document was largely ignored, primarily because our dioceses and parishes were still preoccupied with internal concerns. Pope John Paul II has been tireless in urging the church to what he calls "a *new* evangelization." In his 1990 encyclical letter *The Mission of the Redeemer* he wrote, "The number of those who do not know Christ and do not belong to the Church is constantly on the increase." Then he made his now-famous statement, "I sense that the moment has come to commit *all of the Church's energies* to a new evangelization" (n. 3; emphasis mine). Besides missionary activity among those who do not yet know Christ, the pope is deeply concerned about the many "cultural" Catholics who have been baptized but neither evangelized nor catechized. They have little or no awareness of their faith or its implications for daily life. These are in need of "foundational" evangelization or "re-evangelization."

We cannot conclude this historical survey without noting the pioneering work of Paulist Father Alvin Illig. He spent the last years of his life speaking and writing about evangelization with zeal, wisdom, and good humor that were contagious. It is to him that I credit my own awakening to evangelization. Along with him and his fellow Paulists, Frs. Frank DeSiano and Kenneth Boyack, the U.S. Bishops' Committee on Evangelization held consultations around the country. They came to realize that Catholics in the United States were not responding to papal calls to evangelization, not because of ill will, but mostly because they lacked a clear understanding of what evangelization is or how to go about it. They were being exhorted but not empowered. Finally, in 1992, the bishops published their document *Go and Make Disciples*, subtitled "A National Pastoral Plan and Strategy for Catholic Evangelization in the U.S." In a brief but comprehensive manner, the bishops present a simple and appealing vision of evangelization, together with a set of concrete, practical goals and strategies to help individuals as well as parishes in their evangelizing mission. We will be referencing this document frequently in the remainder of this book.

A
Vision
for
Evangelization

"What *is* evangelization anyway?" That is the question I keep hearing from Catholics every time I start using the "e-word." Understandably so. For reasons noted in the previous chapter, the word had practically disappeared from our Catholic vocabulary. Evangelization was something "those other churches do." Because it is weighted with so much confusion and negative imagery, some people have suggested we simply not use the word; we should use something like "sharing faith" instead. I considered that possibility myself, but rejected it. The word has too long a history to be dismissed. I prefer to use the word as an opportunity to educate and motivate, much as we have done with words like "stewardship" and "Paschal Mystery." Those words were unfamiliar to Catholics too, but with time and education they have become second nature in our conversations.

I like to begin by stating what evangelization is *not*. First, it is not *shaming people into conversion*. We do not want Catholics to go around badgering people with questions like: "Are you saved?" "Have you been born again?" "Have you given your life to Jesus Christ?" We reject all such heavy-handed and intrusive tactics. We do not want to embarrass anyone—or ourselves—in our evangelizing efforts. We favor evangelization that is low-key, gentle, respectful of the beliefs and feelings of all people. Whenever I speak to groups of Catholics for the first time about this topic, I can always see looks of relief in the audience when I assure them that they do not have to do "in-your-face" evangelization.

Second, evangelization is not *"sheep-stealing" from other faiths*. That is, we are not about to go around telling our Protestant, Jewish, or Muslim neighbors that they cannot be saved unless they become Catholic. In the first place, such a statement would be theologically false. Besides, it would sabotage all the hard work of ecumenism that has been building over the past few decades. If someone is already a devoted, practicing member of another religion or denomination, we honor and respect their commitment. If the situation seems appropriate, we may engage them in dialogue, asking about their beliefs and sharing with them our faith in Jesus Christ and why we value our place in the Catholic community. In a word, evangelization does not involve a return to the old-time religious wars. It is not "trying to make everyone Catholic."

Third, evangelization does not mean *engaging in "biblical shoot-outs."* That is, you try to prove the other person wrong by quoting a scripture text; he or she, in turn, quotes one back at you; you come up with another—and so on. I often tell Catholics, "First of all, we will always end up losing—simply because we don't know the Bible that well." But more important, these exchanges do nothing but create arguments and hard feelings—defeating the very purpose of evangelization. Even if we win the battle, we will lose the war. Catholics often feel inadequate to evangelize because they have very few biblical verses or passages memorized. But the truth is, we can be effective evangelizers even without a lot of biblical quotes. I will say more about this later.

And fourth, evangelization is not *trying to fill up our empty pews*. I say this because sometimes parishes try to measure their success in evangelizing by the number of returnees or new candidates for the RCIA. While not a bad idea in itself, this approach can lead us astray. On the one hand, if our numbers are high, we may be tempted to credit ourselves or our methods, whereas Pope Paul VI reminds us that "the Holy Spirit is the principal agent of evangelization. . . . Without the Holy Spirit, the most convincing dialectic has no power over the human heart" (*On Evangelization . . .*, n. 75). On the other hand, if our numbers are meager, we will be tempted to become discouraged or even to give up our evangelizing efforts.

Numbers are one factor to consider. But our primary motivation for evangelizing is simply this: Jesus Christ asked us—commanded us—to do so. In both Matthew's and Mark's gospels, the very last words of Jesus on earth are the commission of the disciples to evangelize: "All power in heaven and on earth has been given to me. Go, therefore, and make disciples of all nations, baptizing them in the name of the Father, and of the Son, and of the holy Spirit, teaching them to observe all that I have commanded you. And behold, I am with you always, until the end of the age" (Mt 28:18-20). It's like Jesus is saying, "Don't let this die. Everything I've done in your midst—my teachings, my miracles, my suffering and dying, my rising from the dead—don't let it be forgotten. Tell everyone about it. Invite them into the community of disciples. And don't be afraid—you won't be alone. I will be with you—through the Holy Spirit—until the very end of time."

So this is our primary motive for evangelizing: obedience to the Lord Jesus. We leave success or failure, high numbers or low, up to him. I find it stunning that Christ has so much confidence in us that he entrusts the spread of his gospel to the likes of us. I once saw a cartoon drawing of the ascension scene described above. The disciples are looking up at Jesus and saying, "But Lord, what if we fail? Do you have a back-up plan?" And Jesus answers, "No—all I have is you!"

Growing in Our Own Faith

Now that we've seen what evangelization is *not*, we are ready to take a look at what it *is*. In the very first place, it means *growing in our own relationship with Jesus Christ*. We ourselves are in constant need of *being* evangelized. Together with our fundamentalist brothers and sisters, we Catholics believe it is necessary to make a personal commitment and have a personal relationship with the Lord Jesus. But we also believe that that commitment and relationship needs to be nourished and strengthened. As Pope Paul VI said, our faith "runs the risk of perishing from suffocation or starvation if it is not fed and sustained each day" (*On Evangelization . . .* , n. 54). Which is why we need to pray, to read the scriptures, to participate in the eucharist and the other sacraments, to continue to study and reflect on the truths of our faith, and to share with other believers who are trying to grow in their spiritual life. It always pains me when I see Catholics who eagerly attend continuing education seminars and workshops to keep up with their professional life, but do little or nothing for their spiritual life. We will be able to evangelize others only if we are both knowledgeable and enthusiastic for the good news of the gospel.

Second, evangelization means *living our faith in action.* Recall what we said in Chapter 1 about how the church grew in the first centuries. Christians gave witness to their newfound faith in Christ by living an exemplary lifestyle. Their neighbors could not help noticing how involved they were in family and civic affairs, yet refrained from the sinful excesses of their contemporaries—and all with a spirit of joy and peacefulness. Pope Paul VI called this "wordless witness." Even in our own time, he says, "these Christians stir up irresistible questions in the hearts of those who see how they live." Questions like: Why are they like this? What or who is it that inspires them? What is the secret of their happiness and graciousness? It makes people think, the pope says—whether they are unbelievers, nominal Christians, or people who are searching for something to believe in. Then he makes the strong statement that "All Christians are called to this witness, and in this way they can be real evangelizers" (*On Evangelization . . .* , n. 21). I can't help thinking of the many people I know who are doing this silent kind of evangelization—in their families, their workplaces, shopping malls, recreation events—and those suffering in hospitals or confined to care centers. Many of us have heard inspiring stories of people who have been brought to faith in Christ or returned to church because of the example of one or two believers. As Ronald Rolheiser says in his wonderful book *The Holy Longing* (Doubleday, 1999), the best way we can make Jesus known to others is not by passing out pamphlets or holding big rallies, but by radiating his compassion and love—in our faces and in our actions (p. 102).

Third, evangelization means *sharing our faith with others*. While wordless witness and good example are necessary, they are not always sufficient for true evangelization. Those who observe *how* we live will sometimes want to know *why*. So they will ask—and we need to be ready to tell them. St. Peter noted this already in the first century when he wrote to the Christians: ". . . [S]anctify Christ as Lord in your hearts. Always be ready to give an explanation to anyone who asks you for a reason for your hope, but do it with gentleness and reverence" (1 Pt 3:15-16a). Or, as Pope Paul VI put it, "The Good News proclaimed by the *witness* of life sooner or later has to be proclaimed by the *word* of life" (*On Evangelization* . . . , n. 22).

But, as I mentioned earlier, Catholics have become "bashful" about sharing their faith. Later on I will offer some simple and effective ways of doing this. For now, here is just one example. At a men's retreat I was giving a few years ago, one of the men told me he had recently returned to the church. I'm always on the lookout for stories like this, so I asked him to tell me what happened. He said he had gone through a job loss and then a divorce—both related to alcohol abuse. He reacted by blaming God and quitting the church. Eventually he sought treatment and began attending an A.A. group that met on Sunday mornings. One day a woman came late to the meeting. "Sorry I'm late," she said in a cheery voice, "but I've just been to church, and it was wonderful!" After the meeting my friend sought her out. "What was so great about church?" he asked. She told him about the beautiful music and how the priest had given an inspiring sermon and how warm and friendly the people were. He said, "Where is that church?" She told him; he went the next Sunday, talked to the priest after Mass, and began his journey of reconciliation with the church. All because someone said, "I was at church today—and it was wonderful!" What a simple way to share one's faith.

Extending an Invitation

Fourth, evangelization means *inviting others to faith.* It is a basic fact that most people will not take the initiative or make the first move toward faith in Christ or connection with the church. There are exceptions, of course, as the above story illustrates. The man was ready, motivated to follow up on the woman's remark about church. But in most cases, after hearing her describe her experience at Mass, he would have said, "That's interesting," rather than "Where is that church?" So, if she was a tuned-in evangelizer, she would have put out a gentle invitation: "The church is Saint So-and-So; it's located at . . . ; would you like to come next week?" Other invitations are even more basic: "It sounds like you're on a spiritual search. Do you ever pray about this?" Or: "Our parish has an inquiry class for people who have questions like yours; would you like to check it out?" Invitations can take many forms. But recall the line we quoted above from St. Peter about speaking gently and respectfully. Invitations should never be heavy-handed or coercive. The person may simply not be ready for any action as yet. But you have lost nothing by extending the invitation. And you have planted a seed which may sprout in God's own time.

Transforming Society

Fifth, evangelization means *working to transform society with gospel values.* The point here is that the cultural environment needs to be evangelized, not merely the individuals within that culture. It is very difficult to maintain a Christian lifestyle if the society all around us is un-Christian. Pope Paul VI said that sometimes the gospel will challenge—even upset—the fashions, values, and role models of the prevailing culture (*On Evangelization* . . . , n. 19). So Christians will have to be engaged in some kind of cultural analysis: discerning which values of the culture should be affirmed because they are in harmony with the gospel, and which should be challenged because they are opposed to it. Evangelizers need to be ready to work together with all people of good will in order to promote whatever favors human dignity and human rights, and to resist whatever is unjust, immoral, and degrading.

Given these five descriptions of evangelization, I would contend that we Catholics are probably evangelizing a good deal more than we realize. I believe, for example, that we are quite serious about trying to grow in our relationship with Christ and generally try to live our faith by way of good example. And certainly, we Catholics are well known for our involvement in social justice, human rights, reverence for life, and concern for the poor. Where we are deficient, though, is in the fact that we do not readily share our faith (we keep it to ourselves), and we do not invite others to take a look at what we have found (we're afraid of being regarded as "pushy" or "fanatical"). I will return to these points later on. At this point it might be helpful to give "a working definition" of evangelization: *"The ongoing endeavor to grow in our own faith and conversion to Jesus Christ; to make known the good news of Christ to others; and to work with all people of good will to transform society with the values of Christ."*

Understood in this way, evangelization is a large concept indeed. Note some of the elements. First, it is "an ongoing endeavor." That means it is not a time-limited program like a retreat or a renewal. Second, it aims first of all at ourselves: it calls us to lifelong conversion and growth in our relationship with Jesus Christ. We constantly need to hear the gospel and respond to it in faith. But third, we are not content to keep the gospel to ourselves; "the love of Christ impels us," as St. Paul says, to make him known to others. And fourth, evangelization includes working to form a more just and caring society according to God's plan for human life.

Who Are We Trying to Reach?

The short answer would be: everyone. Recall what Pope Paul VI said: Every human being has a right to at least hear the gospel of Jesus Christ. But for purposes of discussion we can break down "everyone" into two subgroups: 1) active, practicing Catholics; and 2) all other persons. In their 1992 document on evangelization, the U.S. bishops ask us to direct our evangelizing efforts to active, practicing Catholics. This is for two reasons: first, because their faith needs constant nourishment and upbuilding. It is no secret that many of our church-going people do not show much enthusiasm for their faith. They are often hard-working, responsible, basically good people. But there is no heart, no joy in their religion. They belong to the vast army of Sunday Catholics, dutifully plodding along on the way to salvation. And second, active Catholics have the best chance of reaching the spiritually lost and troubled people of our time. However, by and large we have not encouraged or taught our people how to share their faith with others. Yet all the research shows that most people turn to Christ or connect with a church community because some believer(s) inspired them, befriended them, and shared their faith with them. If we could manage to get this "vast army" fired up, enthused about the treasure of their faith, what a spiritual impact they could have on the whole society.

Which brings us to the other large "target group" for evangelization: the many people who do not know Jesus Christ; or if they do, they are not connected to any faith community. This latter group includes some eighteen million baptized Catholics who no longer practice their faith, plus about eighty million Americans who are "unchurched"—uninvolved with any community of believers. Sociologists speak of the modern religious phenomenon of "believing without belonging." And George Gallup describes such people as "spiritual loners." Our U.S. bishops remind us: We cannot be satisfied with "saving the saved." We are by nature a missionary church. The gathered community (at the eucharist) is called to reach out to the ungathered. Here it is helpful to make a distinction between "seekers" and "satisfied." The latter are people who are disconnected from any church and are content to remain so (at least for now); seekers are those who are disconnected but are still open, still searching for something to believe in and/or a community to belong to. In any case, the evangelizing field is "ripe for the harvest" (Jn 4:35).

Types of Seekers

Let's take a look at some examples of "spiritual seekers." The first group that comes to mind is baptized Catholics who have just drifted away from church and sacraments. They are not hostile, not antagonistic. If you'd ask them why they no longer attend, they would likely say they just "got too busy." They are working hard to advance their careers; their children are involved in all sorts of extra activities; they do a lot of entertaining; they may be looking after aging parents. On Sundays they like to play golf or go skiing, work out at the health club, work in the yard or garden, visit with friends, visit the art museum or attend a sporting event. Sunday Mass doesn't fit into the schedule. And yet, at some level of awareness, they are not totally happy with this pattern. They know or feel that something is out of harmony: they are not giving priority to

God. Sometimes they are stung when their children say, "Our friends always go to church on Sunday. Why don't we?" It is that tweak, that sting, perhaps a bit of nostalgia, that makes them seekers. They would be open to a spiritual conversation, or even an invitation to reconnect with the parish—but they will not make the first move.

Another group: those who were baptized Catholic but had little or no instruction in the faith. They still call themselves Catholic, but they never formed the habit of participating in the church's worship or sacramental life; nor was it modeled in their family of origin. But now they have children of their own, and they feel a desire to pass on some kind of faith to their children. Like the first group, they are seekers, but they will not take initiative in the search. But if someone (Mormon, Jehovah's Witness, Christian fundamentalist, evangelizing Catholic) would connect and issue an invitation, they would probably respond positively. A subgroup here would be those Catholics who have drifted away and are still reluctant to return, but do want some religious formation for their children. I consider them seekers because often, if we begin to catechize their children, they will eventually become active in the church themselves.

A third group are those Catholics who have been divorced. Even if they have not remarried, a surprising number of these believe (wrongly, of course) that they are excommunicated. If and when they learn that this is not the case, many will eagerly reconnect with the church—provided they are made to feel welcome. The more difficult cases are those wherein the Catholic has remarried outside the church. Many would be eligible for an annulment of their previous marriage, but some are reluctant to initiate the process. Sometimes the fee is an obstacle; other times it is fear of reopening old wounds, or of having to face the former spouse. (The latter is a non-issue, because canon law requires only that the other spouse be contacted by letter from the diocese and invited to respond; if he or she chooses not to, the process continues anyway. In any case, there is never any need for a face-to-face meeting). Another groundless fear is that annulment implies that the children born of the previous marriage will be considered illegitimate. The truth is: canon law regards children born of any marriage contracted in good faith (i.e., *at the time*, the marriage was presumed to be valid) to be legitimate. Granted, the annulment process can be tedious and somewhat painful; but the vast majority of petitioners report that it proved to be a healing experience for them, spiritually and emotionally.

Another group of seekers: those who are angry at the church for whatever reason. For some, the changes after Vatican II were too many and too rapid; for others, they were too few and too slow. Others feel unable to accept some of the teachings or policies. Still others have been hurt by the treatment they experienced from priests, sisters, or lay people representing the parish. Perhaps they were scolded in the confessional. Or they were told that their child could not receive one of the sacraments, or attend the school, or have a church wedding. Or the priest failed to visit their sick parent in the hospital or was not available to them in some other way. Perhaps their work in the parish was criticized or not appreciated. Such people are feeling wounded or at least disappointed by the church, so they choose to disconnect. But again, they are not satisfied being "on the outside." They are still seeking a place, hoping for reconciliation. Given the opportunity, they would welcome a conversation with a compassionate member of the parish or pastoral team, though they are not likely to initiate it.

So far we have been describing only baptized but non-practicing Catholics. But there is another large number of seekers who are not connected to any religious body or are no longer active in any. They may be non-practicing Protestants, Jews, or Muslims as well as people who have never belonged to any formal religion. Some of them may have been among the spiritually "satisfied" for many years, spiritual loners who do not feel any need for a communal connection. But now they have been hit with one of the thousand ways that life can hurt us. They are diagnosed with a serious illness, they lose their job, one of their children is arrested or is hurt in an accident, they lose their driver's license for drunken driving, they (or their spouse) are caught having an affair, or one of their loved ones dies prematurely. Suddenly, they find themselves under heavy stress and without spiritual resources to sustain them through the crisis. Where can they turn? Where is the safety net when they are in free-fall? Stripped of their self-sufficiency, their need for God and for grounding in some spiritual tradition and community becomes painfully evident. They become spiritual seekers, open to evangelization.

One final group of seekers: people who are not Catholic—perhaps not Christian either—but feel drawn to the Catholic Church for whatever reason. History and biography are filled with examples of people like this. Whether it be the church's history and continuity, or its long intellectual tradition, or the splendor of its art and architecture, or its solemn ritual, or its structures of authority, or its works on behalf of the poor and downtrodden, or the example of its saints, past and present—something attracts people to want to examine it closely and personally. At the same time, they may be repelled by some of the church's claims and teachings—especially in areas of morality. And they may be put off by its tendency toward abuse of power and authority. Whether such people will actually pursue their search will depend on whether they can find committed believers who will listen respectfully to their concerns and put them in touch with resources that will aid them in their quest.

In this chapter we have taken a closer look at the meaning of evangelization—what it is not as well as what it is. We have also described what Pope Paul VI called "the beneficiaries of evangelization," that is, the various groups of people whom we are trying to reach through our evangelizing efforts. The fact is, there are huge numbers of people in our contemporary American society who have little real knowledge of the gospel of Jesus Christ; or, if they do, have largely forgotten or ignored it. We can no longer take for granted that we are living in "a Christian culture." In fact, many observers now speak more commonly of a "post-Christian" culture or a "de-Christianized" society, which is why Pope John Paul II has been speaking so insistently about the need for "a new evangelization" for our times. There are large cohorts of the population that are simply not being reached by our ordinary forms of parish and diocesan ministry.

At the same time, there are significant numbers of people who would be receptive to the gospel message, if only it were offered in attractive and life-affirming ways, and by evangelizers who are both humanly gracious and spiritually faith-filled. Pope Paul VI expressed it so beautifully when he wrote in his apostolic letter: "The world which, paradoxically, despite innumerable signs of the denial of God, is nevertheless searching for him in unexpected ways and painfully experiencing the need of him—the world is calling for evangelizers to speak to it of a God whom the evangelists themselves should know and be familiar with as if they could see the invisible" (*On Evangelization . . .* , n. 76). "The God whom the evangelists know . . . as if they could see the invisible." There is the spiritual challenge for all of us. Our evangelizing efforts will be effective only insofar as we ourselves are grounded in the knowledge and love of God. Otherwise, evangelization will only be another form of manipulation or ego-enhancement. "Without this mark of holiness," the pope says in the same section, "our word will have difficulty in touching the heart of modern man."

What

Is

"The Good News"?

FOUR

Earlier we described evangelization as bringing the good news of Jesus Christ to the people of our time. We Christians speak so easily—almost unthinkingly— about the gospel as "good news." But what does that really mean? Could it be possible that the gospel is no longer "news," because it has become "old hat," or stale, or trite? Have we heard it so often that it no longer moves and shakes us? Or—could it be that it is not perceived any more as "good" news? Perhaps our presentation of the gospel has focused too much on the bad news of human sinfulness and the impending judgment of God.

Our American bishops clearly do not believe that. In their pastoral plan for evangelization they insist that "the gospel message gives us a different vision of what life is about":

> We do not see a world of blind forces ruled by chance, but a universe created to share God's life; we know that following Jesus means we begin to share God's life here and now. We do not view life's purpose as the gathering of power or riches, but as the gracious invitation to live for God and others in love. We do not calculate what we think

is possible, but know the Spirit of God always makes new things possible, even the renewal of humanity. We do not merely look for many years of contented life, but for an unending life of happiness with God. In our faith, we discover God's eternal plan, from creation's first moment to creation's fulfillment in heaven, giving meaning to our human lives. (*Go and Make Disciples*, p. 3)

"This vision," the bishops add, "is the power of the Good News." And they believe that the gospel vision has the power to attract, by its beauty and truth, all who are searching for spiritual meaning.

Another way to phrase the question: What is the basic content of Jesus' preaching and teaching? What is the meaning of his life, death, and resurrection? Why did the early church's witness to Christ have such power to attract and hold people who had so much to lose by accepting him? My own view is this: *The power of the gospel derives from the fact that it addresses people's deepest human needs.* Psychologists and other students of human behavior are not all agreed, of course, on just what are people's "deepest human needs." But I am going to name four of them, and then try to show how the gospel of Christ answers these needs of the human heart and spirit.

1. We need to know that we are worthwhile as persons. We might call this "the need for significance." For some reason, there seems to be built into the human condition a tendency to doubt our significance. Floating somewhere in the back of our minds is the nagging question: *Am I worthwhile? Do I count? Do I have any value apart from my possessions and achievements?* The question stabs like a knife when we see how easily we can be replaced, or when we can't keep up with the competition, or when we fail at some important project. A priest-friend who gives retreats for youth gives the teens an exercise: he asks them to draw up a double list—first, their flaws and negative qualities, and then their good points. Inevitably, he says, they come up with a lengthy list of negatives and only one or two positives.

No doubt this is a phase that most adolescents go through. The tragedy is that so many adults appear to be stuck in feelings of inadequacy. One reason, I suspect, is the culture's emphasis on competitiveness. We are forever comparing and being compared with others, trying to reassure ourselves that we come off better. As children it was our toys, our clothes, our bug collection, our baby sister. As we get older, the game doesn't change but the stakes get higher; now we compare grades, athletic skills, exploits, and friends. Still later, we compare schools attended, degrees achieved, positions held, tastes cultivated, possessions owned.

A certain amount of competition is just plain human and even healthy. It certainly inspires progress and self-improvement. What I am concerned about here is the negative fallout. What about those who can't keep up? Are they any less valuable as human beings because they lost? And what about those who do manage to keep up? What price are they paying in terms of stress-related illnesses, alcohol and drug abuse, strained marriages, divorces, sheer lack of time and energy for things of the spirit? A long-ago popular song put it into one sad line: "I ran so fast that time and youth ran out; I never stopped to think what life was all about."

Another factor in the feeling of insignificance is the culture's obsession with physical appearance. Day after day, glossy magazines and slick television ads hype the message: "Gorgeous people have all the fun!" The purpose, of course, is to induce you to buy the product that will assure you a place in the fun. But what of the vast majority of us who are, by cultural standards of attractiveness, "average"? Or have reached the age where, as Gail Sheehy once said, "everything is a half-inch lower"? Are we doomed to insignificance? What kind of society have we formed where high-priced models are willing to sell their reproductive eggs on the Internet so that rich couples can be assured of having pretty children? Or where kids have to be wearing the latest fashions so they will be accepted as "cool"? And what shall we say of those people whose desperate need for fame and significance drives them to the grossest forms of exhibitionism on television talk shows?

The gospel and self-worth. Yes, a lot of forces, personal and cultural, combine to create doubts about our own significance and self-worth. So what does the gospel of Jesus Christ have to say about this profoundly human need? I suspect most of us have watched sporting events on television where the camera pans to someone in the audience unrolling a big banner that reads "John 3:16." The act provokes bemused smiles for the most part, but I always see it as a neat form of evangelization. The text cited is a powerful piece of good news: "For God so loved the world that he gave his only Son, so that everyone who believes in him might not perish, but might have eternal life." What it's saying is: God is not a remote, detached observer of our world and our human condition. Rather, God thinks so highly of us, cares so deeply about us, that he desires to share completely in our lives. God went so far as to become one of us when he took on human form in the person of Jesus Christ. Never again can we say: "What does God know about the struggles of human life— about poverty, or hard work, or hunger, or weariness, or fear, or discouragement, or loneliness, or rejection, or betrayal, or painful suffering—and finally, of death?" Because of the mystery we call "the Incarnation," God taking on human flesh, we have to say: God knows and understands all of the above, because of what Jesus experienced. He became like us in every way except sin, the Bible says (see Hebrews 2:17, 4:15).

Now that in itself is enough to make us pause and reflect on our significance as humans. How can we demean ourselves or others if God has embraced our humanness so totally? But Jesus knew that we would need to see and hear that message of dignity in a number of modalities before we would "get it." So during his lifetime he went out of his way to assure us of our basic goodness and significance. "Are not two sparrows sold for a small coin?" he said. "Yet not one of them falls to the ground without your Father's knowledge. Even all the hairs of your head are counted. So do not be afraid; you are worth more than many sparrows" (Mt 10:29-31). Notice that Jesus says we can be free of shame and fear because God holds us in such high regard. Spiritual writer John Shea says that one of our deepest fears is that we are forgettable. But Jesus assures us that we will not be forgotten by God, who does not forget even the lowly sparrows.

Jesus gave us that assurance not only through his teachings but also through his actions. Time after time we see him in the gospels reaching out in love and care to every class of people, including those who were regarded (and regarded themselves) as insignificant. He praised the poor widow who made her small contribution to the temple treasury. He joined himself at table with those who were regarded as sinners. He brought healing to the feared lepers, even touching them and thereby making himself ritually unclean for temple worship. He spoke to women in public, something unheard of for his time and culture. He welcomed children—the ultimate insignificants—embraced them and blessed them. In a thousand ways he tried to communicate the message: "You are worthwhile, you are precious in the eyes of God—every one of you." Even sinners were not left out. His word to them was: "You are forgiven. You can change. You have another chance."

All this is truly good news for our spirits. To us, to the people of our time, to everyone struggling with feelings of inadequacy, with fragile self-esteem, with doubts about self-worth, Jesus speaks the same liberating word: "It doesn't matter if you don't have a lot of possessions or status or good looks. It doesn't matter how far up or down you are on the social ladder. You are the beloved son or daughter of God. You are my sister or my brother. Nothing and nobody can take that away from you."

Question: Is significance acquired (by our achievements), or is it bestowed (as a gift)? My answer: it is both. How many people, suffering acutely from a lack of self-confidence, have found self-worth and significance when they finally discovered they had some recognizable gifts and talents, they could do some things well? This is why parents, educators, and others have such a vital role in helping young people to stretch themselves, to discover their abilities, to test their limits. Indeed, whatever we can do to enable people to find and utilize their potential is a form of sacred activity. But always, underneath and above all accomplishments, is the deeper truth: we are already blessed, already accepted by One who loves us unconditionally. This is not our own doing, St. Paul reminds us; it is God's gracious gift (Eph 2:8).

Self-worth and humility. But a healthy sense of self-esteem is not a sinful form of pride, either. It is instructive to recall that St. Thomas Aquinas once defined humility as "the reasonable pursuit of one's own excellence." We can hardly find a more psychologically refreshing statement. It asserts that we do have a God-given excellence and we are called to develop it by making use of our abilities in accord with reason, balance, and good judgment. Pride, on the other hand, is the unreasonable pursuit of our excellence. This may take various forms: boasting of our accomplishments, real or otherwise; exalting ourselves while belittling others; driving ourselves to the point of neglecting our health, our family, or other important values. Perhaps the best "formula" for growing in our sense of significance is this combination: belief in our basic goodness *plus* a passion for self-improvement. Without the former, the latter will degenerate into a compulsive drive to prove oneself. Without the latter, the former will become self-satisfied complacency.

My dream is that the church will proclaim this great truth of our significance in ever more convincing ways. The gospel does insist that we are not only graced but also flawed. We are, at one and the same time, holy and sinful. We are in need of conversion, up to the very moment of death. At the human level, too, we are limited. There are some things we will not be able to accomplish. We are going to fail, make mistakes, commit sins. We need to understand and accept this "shadow" side of ourselves if we are ever going to experience the full reality of God's redemptive love. Lewis Smedes puts it so well when he writes: "The point is that the grace of God comes to us in our scrambled spiritual disorder, our mangled inner mass, and accepts us with all our unsorted clutter, accepts us with all our potential for doing real evil and all our fascinating flaws that make us such interesting people. He accepts us totally as the spiritual stew that we are. . . . For the whole shadowed self each one of us is, grace has one loving phrase: You are accepted. Accepted. Accepted. . . ." (*Shame and Grace,* Zondervan, 1993, p. 117). What a wonderful truth for our contemporary world to hear.

I will close this section with a note from the life of St. Francis of Assisi. When he finally heard the gospel message of God's love for him, in spite of his sins and flaws, he wanted everyone to know that the same love was available to them. He would make it a point to greet the people he met with the words, "Good morning, good people!" Now Francis was not naive. He knew that the people he greeted were not all good. But he did know that, like himself, there was a core of goodness in each one that needed to be acknowledged and affirmed. By addressing them as "good people," Francis was saying: "You are a sinner, and so am I. You are unfinished, and so am I. But above all that—you are good, you are enfolded in the love of God, and so am I. Let's begin each day with that joyful awareness, and see how it can transform our lives!"

2. We need to know that we belong (are connected). What good is a feeling of significance if we are all alone? Contemporary social scientists have noted a curious paradox: Today's society provides more opportunities than ever before for people to connect with each other—high mobility, numerous places to gather, clubs and organizations of every kind, the Internet. At the same time, never before have so many people feared being alone. "The lonely crowd" has become almost a metaphor to describe modern society. We can all identify with Charlie Brown's ongoing but futile attempts to connect with "that little red-haired girl." Teenagers panic if they are still romantically unattached after age sixteen. Nearly every major newspaper now includes pages of "Personal" columns wherein people can seek a suitable companion. Computerized dating services are a multi-million dollar industry. People stay in relationships long after they become troubled simply because it's better than being alone. Elderly people often feel they don't belong in a youth-worshipping world and where extended families are spread all over the continent. Even married couples complain of feeling alone: "We don't communicate." "We're too busy with our separate projects." The ache of loneliness is acute indeed.

The sense of belonging, which appears to be a strong human need, has suffered from the breakdown of certain communal systems that used to provide support for individuals. Extended families, often living close to each other; close-knit neighborhoods, where people watched out for one another's children; ethnic parishes with their common language and cultural traditions—all contributed to the feeling of being connected. As people moved out of the old neighborhoods and into the suburbs, much of this was lost. I once heard someone say, "We began to lose our sense of community when architects no longer designed homes with front porches." Interesting. Many of us can remember the days when we used to spend summer evenings sitting on the front porch. Passers-by would be invited to join us for popcorn, lemonade, and conversation. Nowadays people seem to value privacy over community. Neighbors hardly know each other, and family activities take place in the back yard behind a wooden fence.

The gospel and community. In any case, granted that "natural" communities are receding, how does the gospel of Jesus address our human need for belonging and connection? As I stated earlier, Jesus was imbued with the great themes of the Old Testament. One of these was the notion of marriage as a God-given institution. The Book of Genesis describes God as gazing upon the first human creature and saying, "It is not good for the man to be alone. I will make a suitable partner for him" (Gn 2:18). God then proceeded to create woman and presented her to the man as his lifelong companion. Jesus reaffirmed the goodness of this arrangement when he challenged the lawyers of his time to stop permitting divorce (Mk 10:1-12).

At the same time, Jesus did not view marriage as the only form of belonging or the sole remedy for loneliness. He himself renounced marriage and taught that sometimes family ties can get in the way of discipleship. But he went about forming a new community, based on a new covenant. Beginning with his own disciples, he patiently formed them into a community, trying to free them from the petty ambitions and rivalries that threatened to divide them (Mt 20:20-28). He tried to impress on them that membership in the community is not to be based on rank or status or gender or ethnic origin, but solely on the willingness to be his faithful disciples. He prayed that *all* people would eventually be brought together into one human community (Jn 17:20-21). He taught that the distinctive mark of this new community would be nothing other than love: "I give you a new commandment: love one another. As I have loved you, so you also should love one another. This is how all will know that you are my disciples, if you have love for one another" (Jn 13:34-35). And he made it clear that this new community should be one in which repentant sinners can always find a home. "The Son of Man has come to seek and to save what was lost," he said as he invited the despised tax collector Zacchaeus to dine with him (Lk 19:10). As he told the stories of the shepherd looking for the one lost sheep and the father who lovingly welcomed back his wayward son, Jesus taught the church that it is always to be a place—a community—of forgiveness and reconciliation.

When we read the Acts of the Apostles and the New Testament letters, we find that the early church did try to embody Christ's vision of community. We read in Acts that "there was no needy person among them," because the members shared their goods with those who were not as well off (Acts 4:34). The apostles made sure that there would be no discrimination based on language differences when it came to the distribution of food and other necessities for the widows in the community (Acts 6:1-4). A major breakthrough in the vision of community occurred when the apostles finally came to understand that Jesus' church was intended not only for Jews but also for Gentiles—nations and peoples everywhere and of every class (Acts 10 and 15). Very quickly, the celebration of the eucharist ("the Lord's Supper") was seen as both the sign and the instrument of unity—between believers and their risen Lord and among believers themselves. When Paul learned that the Christians at Corinth were practicing forms of discrimination at the eucharist, he was quick to challenge them: "How can you eat the Lord's Supper when there are such divisions among you?" was the essence of his rebuke (1 Cor 11:17-22). In fact, the New Testament writers showed zero tolerance for any form of discrimination, especially toward the poor (see James 2:1-4). The church was to be an inclusive community, where everyone would be welcome and everyone could find a home.

The church and community. Sadly, today's church has not always revealed this face. As individuals and as parishes, we have a long way to go toward creating communities where people will find a sense of welcome and belonging. Granted, the church is not a religious version of group therapy. It is not equipped to meet all our needs for love and intimacy. For that we need our families and some faithful, caring friends. But surely the church is called to be a place of welcome and of healing. I will say more about this later on. But first let me share a personal anecdote.

One Sunday noon another friar and I were about to fly off to our preaching assignments and we were having lunch at a crowded restaurant. At the table next to us was a young couple with two delightful children. It was apparent that the couple was paying some attention to our conversation. Finally they came over to our table and said, "We can't help overhearing your discussion—are you preachers?" "Yes," we said, "we're Catholic priests." "Oh, that's great. We just came from our church—the Assembly of God. Our pastor is so good. He's always telling us that we should confess our sins—isn't that wonderful?" We agreed. "And now he wants to build a school for our children—isn't that wonderful?" Agreement again. "And we have Bible study every week at our church, and it's so good to learn about the Bible. And by the way, we used to be Catholic." At that point I could no longer hold my tongue. "Tell me," I said, "You're so pleased that your pastor urges you to confess your sins. Well, we've always had confession of sins in the Catholic Church. He's hoping to build a school; we've always had parochial schools. And nowadays most of our parishes have Bible classes for adults. Could you tell me: What are you finding in this church that you were not finding as Catholics?" Fair question, I thought. But the answer surprised me. It was not about theology, or scripture, or authority. It was simply about the sense of belonging. "The Catholic Church is so cold," they said with much feeling. "Nobody talks to you. After Mass the people rush out to the parking lot and nearly run you over on the way out. At this church, everybody says, 'Hi, great to see you here. Have you met the pastor? Have you met so-and-so—they're in charge of this-and-that program if you'd like to be part of it. And we have Bible classes for your children.' It's just so much warmer and friendlier than the Catholic Church." I didn't know what to say because I could not deny their experience. But I began to realize: What they are asking for is not that difficult, not unreasonable. Surely, with all our resources and with a little imagination, we can make our parishes places of warmth, welcome, and hospitality—closer to what I believe Jesus envisioned. Once again, the gospel speaks to one of our human needs: the need to belong, to be connected, to be at home.

3. We need to know that we have a purpose for living. Human beings are the only species that are concerned about the meaning and purpose of their lives. Plants and animals don't worry about this; their instincts guide them toward simple survival and propagation of their species. But humans possess that awesome capacity to ask questions like: "Why are we here? What is the meaning of our lives? Do we have any larger purpose than survival—and death?" "Is that all there is, my friend?"

It is often said that we are living in a "postmodern" culture, where the prevailing philosophy is nihilism. Meaning: there is no objective truth, no moral absolutes, no coherence or meaning to life. There is really nothing to believe in beyond fate. Life is basically absurd. Deal with it. In such a culture, the basic attitude is cynicism. It is fashionable to knock and ridicule everything. Being irreverent is cool. We see these attitudes reflected in much of today's popular culture—movies, TV shows, music. Nothing is really worth striving for, so just get all you can for yourself while you can.

But some have glimpsed the dead end here. Popular actor Brad Pitt was quoted recently as saying, "I'm the guy who's got everything. But I'm telling you: once you've got everything, then you're just left with yourself." Interesting insight. I recall a couple of years ago when President Clinton was having a press conference with a group of young people. The only soundbite the media bothered to show was the young guy who asked the president what kind of shorts he wears—boxers or briefs. But someone told me about a profound question left unreported by most of the media. It was from seventeen-year-old Dahlia Schweitzer who asked: "Mr. President, it seems to me that [rock star] Kurt Cobain's recent suicide exemplified the emptiness that many in my generation feel. How do you propose to teach our young how valuable life is?" The usually articulate president was at a loss for words. He made some reference to his bill in Congress to help families, and then called on the next raised hand. But Ms. Schweitzer's question hung in the air like a cloud that wouldn't evaporate.

"How do you propose to teach our young people how valuable life is?" The agonizing question can be reframed: In today's "deconstructed" world, how can we find meaning for our lives? Rabbi Harold Kushner tapped into this human need in his book *When All You've Ever Wanted Isn't Enough* (Simon & Schuster, 1986). Early in the book he says: "Our souls are not hungry for fame, comfort, wealth, or power. Those rewards create almost as many problems as they solve. Our souls are hungry for meaning, for the sense that we have figured out how to live so that our lives matter, so that the world will be at least a little bit different for our having passed through it" (p. 18). A few pages later he adds that the question of whether life has meaning and purpose is a religious question—not because it has to do with church-going but because it is about ultimate values and concerns.

The gospel and the purpose of life. So what does the gospel of Jesus have to say about the purpose of life? Some of his familiar sayings take on fresh meaning when heard in terms of what life is really all about:

🕊 To those who believe life is about acquiring more he says: "Do not store up for yourselves treasures on earth, where moth and decay destroy, and thieves break in and steal. But store up treasures in heaven, where neither moth nor decay destroy, nor thieves break in and steal. For where your treasure is, there also will your heart be" (Mt 6:19-21). "Treasures in heaven" are spiritual goods that are acquired through a life focused on honoring God and caring for others.

🕊 To those who believe life is about caring only for themselves, Jesus calls instead for a life of service to others. At the Last Supper he kneels down and washes the feet of his disciples, a task traditionally performed by servants. Afterward he explains: "Do you realize what I have done for you? You call me 'teacher' and 'master,' and rightly so, for indeed I am. If I, therefore, the master and teacher, have washed your feet, you ought to wash one another's feet. I have given you a model to follow. . . ."

(Jn 13:12-15). Jesus sees "washing feet" as a metaphor for humble service of one another. And he wanted that attitude of service to be prominent even—and especially—in the minds of those who exercise authority in the community. It was to be the very antithesis of power-seeking. Earlier he had told the twelve apostles, "whoever wishes to be great among you shall be your servant; whoever wishes to be first among you shall be your slave. Just so, the Son of Man did not come to be served but to serve and to give his life as a ransom for many" (Mt 20:26-28). Here Jesus undercuts the jockeying for rank and position that can so often poison the community. And the last sentence highlights another clear gospel value:

🕊 To those who think life is about comfort and self-indulgence, Jesus reminds his followers of the absolute necessity of self-denial, bearing the cross daily, and being willing to give up one's own life for his sake (Lk 9:23-24).

All this is truly a different, counter-cultural vision of the purpose of life. Life is about honoring God, not glorifying ourselves. It is about sharing with others, not piling up more for ourselves; about caring for others, not looking out for ourselves; about serving others, not seeking power over them; about generosity and self-sacrifice, not protecting our own self-interest and staying in our comfort zone.

But in what sense is this "good news"? It can sound pretty grim. And here precisely is the problem with the gospel of Jesus Christ. It may not make sense, logically or psychologically. This part of the gospel often does not speak to people who are still in the developmental stage of "finding" themselves or "establishing" themselves—typically, adolescents and young adults. They are more attracted by the gospel's answer to the first two human needs I noted: the need for significance and the need for belonging and acceptance. But the need for meaning and purpose seems to emerge at a later stage of human development: middle age and later. At that point many people have found their identity and their talents and their place. But now the troublesome question emerges: "What's it all *for*?" As Stephen Covey would say, "Have I climbed the ladder of success only to find that it's leaning against the wrong wall?" (*Seven Habits of Highly Effective People*, p. 98). Is there anything more out there than moving up, pursuing the good life, acquiring more toys, tasting more pleasures, cramming in more experiences?

Well, if we open up to Jesus' vision of the good life, we will not simply drift along with the cultural tide. We will pay attention to that small whisper inside us that keeps saying, "There's got to be something more." St. Paul challenged the Christians of his time: "Do not conform yourselves to this age [the pagan society around you] but be transformed by the renewal of your mind, that you may discern what is the will of God, what is good and pleasing and perfect" (Rom 12:2). In other words, accept the vision of Jesus and bring your daily life into conformity with it. Those first Christians came to believe they were called to *make a difference* in the world by their manner of living. Jesus had asked them to become "salt for the earth and light for the world" (see Matthew 5:13-14)—not just "blend in." So they came to see that the primary purpose of their life was to help bring about what Jesus called "the reign of God" in this world. Indeed, that was their *mission*: to create a new society, one based on love and service, not greed and violence.

A sense of mission. But how to do this? The gospel does not give a neat blueprint, but it does give some clear guidelines. In the first place, Christians realized they were called to live an exemplary moral life. Nearly all the New Testament letters remind Christians that their lives must reflect the values that Jesus taught. In

Paul's letter to the Ephesians, for example, he urges his hearers to speak the truth to one another, since lying breaks down trust in the community. They are certain to get angry at times, but they should deal with it, talk it out if necessary, not hold on to it like a grudge. They should refrain from stealing; instead, work to provide for their needs. They should avoid foul language, use their power of speech to encourage and build up, not tear down. And they will be compassionate and kind to one another; if they offend each other, they will ask and grant forgiveness—just as "God has forgiven you in Christ" (Eph 4:32). The idea was: by these daily decisions, these daily acts of love and self-transcendence, Christians will gradually but surely extend the reign of God in the world and become, in Paul's words, "the good fragrance of Christ."

But over and above living a good ethical and moral life, there was another side to the Christians' sense of mission. They noted how Jesus did not attempt to fulfill his mission alone. He enlisted the help of his disciples (Mt 10:1; 28:16-20; Mk 16:15, 20). He had confidence in them and endowed them with spiritual power for evangelizing and healing. So Christians came to realize that they were called to use their gifts and abilities in service of the community. They were convinced that, through their baptism and confirmation, they also were blessed with spiritual gifts that would contribute to building up the entire "body of Christ" (which was Paul's favorite image for the church). Some will have the gift of teaching; others, evangelizing; others, leadership and administration; others, compassionate listening; others, care for the poor and the sick; still others, generosity with their material resources (see Rom 12:3-8). The role of authority was to call forth these gifts, nurture them, and order them for the good of the whole community.

As time went on, Christians began to understand one other side of mission. Not only were they called to render service to the Christian community; they were also to contribute their skills and talents in the secular arena. Why? Because *all* human life is sacred. All of creation is the arena for God's presence and activity. God's reign is to extend to every aspect of human existence. So the notion of "stewardship" began to include the tasks of farming and baking and carpentry and the making of clothing and the exercise of public office and. . . . When the Christian fulfilled these activities with care and skill and responsibility, he or she was truly fulfilling a mission and extending God's reign in the world.

So here is more "good news" for contemporary persons. According to the gospel, human existence is not absurd or meaningless. We are not an accident of nature, not a blip on the radar screen of life. We have been chosen by God, each one of us, "before the foundation of the world," as Paul says (Eph 1:4). Chosen and placed here by God for a spiritual purpose: to come to know and love God and our neighbor; to help re-create this world in accord with God's plan; to help build a "civilization of love," as Pope John Paul II says, in place of a culture of violence and death. Even if we are not particularly talented, every one of us can contribute in some way to the furthering of God's reign. We can live an exemplary Christian life. We can treat every person with dignity and respect. We can be responsible and conscientious in our work. We can practice the simple, loving gestures of kindness and forgiveness.

Over and above these basic forms of mission, Christians today are becoming aware of a profound biblical truth: God has entrusted the care of our planet, especially its human inhabitants, to us. God has chosen to make us partners in the ongoing mysteries of creation and redemption. For our part, we are to use our talents and abilities to serve the human family. Just as the first Christians found, this can take the form of service either in the church or in the wider society—or both. The shortage of priestly and religious vocations has been the stimulus for so many more lay people to become involved in church ministry. But even if there were an abundance of vocations, we have come to a new consciousness: baptism itself calls every person to some form of ministry or service.

For some, this will involve liturgical ministries such as reader, usher, musician, or eucharistic minister. Others will serve as religion teachers, committee members, financial consultants, or youth ministers. Other people will be drawn to activities that benefit the civic community. They will serve on advisory boards and contribute their expertise in education, health care, management, the pro-life movement, or care for the environment. This is the meaning of "stewardship"—using our God-given abilities to make a positive difference in the human enterprise. For these Christians, their job or volunteer work is not just an occupation; it is a vocation, a call from God, a mission. Which is why I really like one of the prayers of Cardinal John Henry Newman; he titled it "Absolute Trust," but it is also a prayer of mission:

> God has created me to do Him some definite service. He has committed some work to me which He has not committed to another. I have my mission. . . . I have a part in a great work; I am a link in a chain, a bond of connection between persons. He has not created me for naught. I shall do good, I shall do His work; I shall be an angel of peace, a preacher of truth in my own place, while not intending it, if I do but keep His commandments and serve Him in my calling.
>
> Therefore, I will trust Him. . . . (A.N. Wilson, *John Henry Newman: Prayers, Poems, Meditations*, p. 26.)

4. We need hope in the midst of life's pain. Some time ago one of my fellow preachers asked me if I ever read *The National Enquirer*. I thought he was joking, so I said no, I don't have time for such junk. But he pushed me a bit, saying it would give me some idea of where a certain segment of the population focuses their interest. So I bought a copy. To me, the articles were nothing but sensationalist journalism. However, what I found interesting was the Classified Ad section. There I found pitches for products so fantastic that I had to laugh. There were ads promising $1000 by next week (just send $7.50 to the P.O. Box!); a spray guaranteed to make you virtually irresistible to the opposite sex; a cream to prevent premature aging; a psychic promising "immediate results" for resolving personal problems; and a "One Day" divorce by mail. There was even an ad saying, "Become a Catholic Priest. . . . Unnecessary to relocate or abandon present career. Celibacy optional." I almost wrote to see if I would qualify!

But what's going on here? What all these ads are basically selling is *hope*. And I recalled a conversation I had with a businessman who said, "Any company that can sell hope will never go out of business." Unfortunately, hope is not a commodity that can be bought and sold. It is an attitude of spirit, one that is sometimes hard to justify. Where will people find hope when they are told they have an incurable illness? Or when their spouse announces they've found someone else and want a divorce? Or when the family farm has to be sold? Or when a family member commits suicide? These are shocks to the soul for which there is no healing medicine or therapy. "Life is difficult" is the well known opening line of M. Scott Peck's *The Road Less Traveled*. It is also a sober fact of life.

So the final of our four basic human needs is to find hope in the midst of life's pain. Because there is no escape from pain and suffering, we have no choice but to confront it. Some people will become bitter and cynical, railing against fate or against God, whom they blame for life's misfortunes. Others will endure stoically, trying to pretend it doesn't hurt. Others will numb themselves with alcohol or drugs, or distract themselves with a flurry of activity or pleasure-seeking.

The gospel and hope. What does the gospel of Jesus have to say about the hurts of life? As we have seen, the very first response of Jesus to human suffering was to offer healing. Matthew's gospel describes what I like to call "a day in the life of Jesus of Nazareth." After finishing his Sermon on the Mount, Jesus headed for Capernaum, the town he would use as his home base for a while. On the way he was met by a leper who begged to be healed. Jesus reached out, touched him and cured him. Arriving in town, a Roman centurion approached and asked Jesus to heal his paralyzed servant. Jesus did so without even visiting the man's home. Next he cured Peter's mother-in-law who was sick with a fever. Then, toward evening, a large crowd of people from the town came to the house, bringing their sick and suffering loved ones. Jesus moved among them, touching them, expelling the evil spirits and healing the illnesses (Mt 8:1-16; Lk 4:40-41). Clearly, Jesus was deeply moved by human suffering and responded with both compassion and healing power. I once heard a scripture scholar say that fully one-fifth of the gospels are about Jesus' healing ministry. Moreover, he empowered his disciples to continue the ministry (Mt 10:8; Lk 9:1-2; Mk 16:17-18). As a result, not only during his days on earth but also after his return to heaven, people found hope in the midst of suffering (Acts 8:7-8).

But obviously Jesus did not cure everybody who came to him (Mk 6:5), and neither did the disciples (Mt 17:16). What was the source of hope for "the unhealed"? Here we enter into the mystery of the cross. Jesus himself did not escape the pain of suffering a cruel death. The first Christians wrestled with this awful truth. They had to ask themselves: What sustained Jesus, what gave him hope, through those horrible hours of his passion and death? And the answer they came to: it was his confidence in the ultimate faithfulness of God. Contrary to all appearances, God did not abandon Jesus on the cross. Just when death appeared to triumph over this innocent victim, God raised him to life—fullness of life, never to die again. That is our faith. It is the mystery of the death and resurrection of Jesus that finally grounds our hope. As Fr. Patrick Brennan puts it so well: "Hope is really a by-product of something else: a deep, abiding conviction that there is a loving Someone in the midst of all reality ordering all things for the good of us all. Jesus called this Loving Someone 'Father'" (*Paschal Journey*, p. 47).

The New Testament writers were passionate about proclaiming the resurrection of Jesus as the foundation for hope. Christians were living in a hostile, even dangerous environment. Religious and civil authorities saw them as enemies of the established order. Most ordinary citizens of the empire were either suspicious or contemptuous of them. At any moment they could be arrested, have their property confiscated, be imprisoned, or killed. They were in great need of hope. They knew their faith in Christ could not protect them from all harm, from torture or death. Their hope had to go deeper. The same loving God who did not abandon Jesus would not finally abandon them. If called upon to make the ultimate sacrifice of their life, they had to trust that death will not be the final outcome. As with Jesus, their death would be a passing over into new life, fullness of life with God and with other faithful believers.

So these Christians were strengthened in their hope when they heard the words of St. Paul proclaimed in their assemblies: "We know that all things work for good for those who love God. . . . If God is for us, who can be against us?" Therefore, nothing—not hardships, or privations, or fears, or death itself—"will be able to separate us from the love of God in Christ Jesus our Lord" (Rom 8:28, 31, 39). He wrote to the Christians in Corinth about his own afflictions and sufferings in the province of Asia—so severe that he thought he was going to die. But he was delivered by God, in whom "we have put our hope" (2 Cor 1:8-10). He urges them not to give way to discouragement, not even to fear death, because ". . . this momentary light affliction is producing for us an eternal weight of glory beyond all comparison, as we look not to what is seen but to what is unseen; for what is seen is transitory, but what is unseen is eternal" (2 Cor 4:17-18). The letters of Peter likewise encourage Christians to remain in hope despite trials and hardships. He reminds them not to be surprised that "a trial by fire" is taking place among them. Rather, they can rejoice in the knowledge that they are sharing in the sufferings of Christ himself and will share his glory at the end: "As a result, those who suffer in accord with God's will hand their souls over to a faithful creator as they do good" (1 Pt 4:19).

So we see once again that the gospel of Jesus is truly good news for our spirits. With all our advances in medicine and technology, we will never succeed in totally eliminating human pain or escaping the hurts of life. We will always be in need of hope. But our reason for hope is not found in any merely human promise or achievement. Hope is grounded in the faithfulness of God to the divine promises. Jesus never promised to protect us from all pain and heartache. He did promise to *be with us* always, till the end of time (Mt 28:20). He did promise to strengthen and empower us to deal with our trials: "Come to me, all you who labor and are burdened," he said, "and I will give you rest" (Mt 11:28). He promised everlasting life to those who would persevere in their faith and hope till the end (Mt 24:13).

Modern examples of hope. All of us have known people who were possessed of such hope. No matter how many setbacks they have, how many disappointments they suffer, they continue to hope, continue to affirm the goodness of life. "God always seems to come through when we need it the most," they will say. Or, "Jesus bore the cross for us; now it's our turn." I remember being moved by a scene in the movie *Country*. The family is on the verge of losing their farm. The father, unable to deal with the loss, has just beaten up his son in a drunken rage and gone back to the tavern. The mother gathers up all her strength, sits the children down at the supper table and says, "Listen— we're going through some hard times. But we're going to keep this family together. Do you understand? Now, let's say our prayers." Later, as she watches the children sleeping, we see her lips moving in silent prayer as the piano in the background softly plays the melody of "Humbly We Adore Thee." The message is unmistakable: the ultimate source of this woman's strength is her hope in God.

On a more personal note, I had a friend named Dan whose life was strewn with personal and familial problems. Reacting with anger and self-pity at first, he gradually grew into an attitude of inner peace and trust in God. One autumn a truck pulled out in front of him and he couldn't avoid crashing into it. The driver was killed, and Dan suffered broken limbs. It took him a while to stop blaming himself for the accident. I was stationed out of state at the time, but at Christmas time I went to visit him. I was surprised at his positive attitude, despite the fact that he still couldn't return to work and the family finances were strained. At one point he asked me, "Do you guys still work with the poor?" I assured him we did. He then reached in his pocket and handed me a roll of cash. "Here, use this for them," he said. I protested, "You need that yourself right now. Maybe later. . . ." But he cut me off. "Take it," he insisted, "I've had a good year." How could he call it a good year, I wondered. But in the face of that kind of faith in God, I had no choice but to accept his offer and assure him of God's blessing. Some years later, he was diagnosed with Lou Gehrig's disease. He deteriorated quite rapidly, but maintained his hope in God and his great sense of humor right to the end. He (and his devoted wife) will always be models to me of gospel hope.

To me, then, this is what we're talking about when we say the gospel of Jesus is "good news." It is "good" because it answers the deepest needs and hungers of the human heart: the need for significance, the need for belonging, the need for a sense of purpose in life, and the need to maintain hope. And it is "news" because it is always relevant—at the various ages of life, for people of all backgrounds, and for those of every social condition. That's why I'm so convinced that the gospel message has power to touch the hearts of people of our time. I keep thinking of those many people "out there" who desperately need to hear those liberating words: "You *are* significant and valuable; you *do* have a place in the body of Christ; you *do* have a mission and a purpose; and there *is* reason for hope amid life's pain."

I remember being so moved when Pope John Paul II spoke at the Youth Congress in Denver a few years ago. At one point he looked up from his prepared speech and gazed directly at the huge throng of young people. Then he said: "This is not a time to be ashamed of the gospel. It is a time to be proud of it—to shout it from the housetops!" And his young audience roared their approval.

Evangelizing
Active
Catholics

Most readers of this book will already be convinced of the urgency for evangelization in our time: there are just too many people we are not reaching. They will also agree with what was presented in the last chapter: that the gospel still has appeal to contemporary men and women because it speaks to the deep spiritual and emotional needs of all people. But the key question is: *How* can we best evangelize? What methods or strategies shall we employ in order to reach the people of our time with the gospel message?

The closest thing we have to a "blueprint" for evangelizing is the U.S. Bishops' National Pastoral Plan (*Go and Make Disciples*, USCC, 1993). The bishops first offer a "vision" of Catholic evangelization based on scripture, tradition, and our cultural situation. But then they move on to "goals and strategies" for becoming a more evangelizing church. They clearly want to move us to action. They hope that parish groups will not only study the Plan but will use it to sharpen the parish's mission and develop concrete evangelizing activities. In fact, they say, "These goals are addressed to *all Catholics* in our country" including every individual and every family: "Although everyone will pursue these goals with different gifts, no one can claim exemption from them" (p. 12).

There is an urgency in the bishops' message. It's like they are saying: "We've had enough words, enough documents. It's time to get moving. Our church must not remain bogged down in internal squabbles and disputes. People are hungry for the truth of the gospel, and we're going to offer it to them."

Before presenting their three major goals for evangelization, the bishops make a couple of preliminary points. One is that "these goals are meaningless unless they are steeped in prayer. Without prayer, the Good News of Jesus Christ cannot be understood, spread, or accepted." So individuals and the entire parish "must ask unceasingly for the grace to evangelize" (p. 12). The moment we try to do it merely with our own human ingenuity, we will fail miserably. This is why, when I begin helping parishes with evangelization, I ask them to include that intention in their intercessory prayers at Mass and to ask parishioners, including those who are sick or homebound, to pray for the parish's evangelizing mission.

Secondly, the bishops warn against seeing evangelization as something that is done by a few people in the parish while everyone else says, "Let *them* do it." No, evangelization has to be owned and carried out by the entire parish, under the leadership of the pastor. A separate committee or task force is often helpful to spearhead the ministry, but evangelization has to be seen as "the primary and essential mission" of the whole parish, as Pope Paul VI said. I will say more about this later.

We turn now to the first goal envisioned by the Pastoral Plan. The bishops state it this way: *To bring about in all Catholics such an enthusiasm for their faith that, in living their faith in Jesus, they freely share it with others.*

Very interesting. The bishops are saying that WE are the first people who need evangelization: "Clearly, unless we continue to be evangelized ourselves, with renewed enthusiasm for our faith and our Church, we cannot evangelize others." We need to get beyond our shyness and our tendency to keep our faith to ourselves. The bishops remind us that we have so much to be grateful for as Catholics. The Word of God in scripture; the presence of Jesus in the sacraments, especially the eucharist; our rich tradition of teaching, ritual, and prayer; moral guidance for our lives and those of our children; the inspiring example of countless saints; and the hope of eternal life. How many people in our society are hungry for some of this, perhaps without being able to name it? As the bishops say, this heritage calls us to offer it as a legacy, a treasure that God wants to bestow on everyone who is searching (*Go and Make Disciples*, pp. 7-8).

I often wonder how many Catholics think of their faith as "a legacy" or "a treasure." Or how often they reflect, dwell on those great truths of our faith that the bishops have named, and let themselves be animated and inspired. I wish I could see more evidence of "enthusiasm" among our Catholics. Some, of course, will say, "How can I be enthused when I see how church officials treat people, how they try to stifle creative thinking? Or when I see how the number of priests is shrinking, while the Vatican refuses to consider ordaining women and married men?" Those are painful questions indeed. The only reply I can think of is to remind myself that the church has never been fully what it ought to be. If we insist on waiting till the church becomes free of all its imperfections before we begin evangelizing—we will never begin. There is no reason why we cannot share with others our faith in the Lord Jesus and at the same time keep working to change structures and practices within the church that are not in keeping with the gospel.

The Importance of Preaching

What are some concrete strategies that could help active Catholics become more enthused about their faith? I would start with preaching. After all, "faith comes from what is heard," as St. Paul says (Rom 10:17). Willow Creek Community Church in South Barrington, Illinois, is probably the fastest-growing Christian church in the nation right now. The founding pastor, Bill Hybels, tells how the church began. He went door-to-door in the town of Palatine and asked people, "Do you regularly attend a local church? If not, would you be willing to tell me why?" People were, and they did. The three most common reasons for non-attendance were: 1) the worship was lifeless and boring; 2) there was too much talk about money; and 3) the sermons were irrelevant to daily life. As one put it: "Preachers talked about issues that have nothing to do with my life. They never even mention the kinds of struggles that I'm going through: a marriage in turmoil, my oldest son out of control, feeling discouraged." At that point Hybels commented: "If I ever preach an irrelevant sermon, if I ever bore people with the Gospel—drag me out of the ministry. Don't let me do it. It's killing people. It's driving them from the only thing that can lead them to faith." That's the kind of passion preachers need.

I've read and heard so many sermons where the preacher did a superb job of laying out the biblical background for the text, putting the readings into their historical-cultural context, explaining the meaning of certain words from the Greek, and showing how the original hearers probably understood the text or story. But I kept saying to myself, "So what? What does that have to do with people's lives today?" At some point I realized I was often guilty of the same lapse. So I resolved to have the "So what?" question always in the back of my mind as I was composing or preaching a homily. It is really not that difficult. If I keep in mind some of those basic human needs I spoke of in the last chapter, I find that the biblical texts always have something meaningful to say about our human situation here and now.

Liturgy as Evangelizing

It is not only the homily but the entire Sunday Eucharist that can and ought to be an evangelizing experience. Paulist Father Frank DeSiano has a fine book on evangelization entitled *Sowing New Seed* (Paulist Press, 1994). In one chapter he talks about the fact that many of our Catholic people have stopped attending Sunday Mass. The usual reason given is that they find the Mass "boring." And that in spite of all the attempts the church has made to improve the liturgy: the priest faces the people, the prayers are in English, there is much more variety in the scripture readings and music, our people are still bored. They're used to television and sports events and live concerts and standup comedians. So some churches try to have dramatic skits and bigger choirs and full-band accompaniment. But, DeSiano says, that is not the answer. The priest may never measure up to Billy Graham or Robert Schuller. The choir may be great, but it can't compete with MTV or the Mormon Tabernacle Choir.

No, the author says, the problem is deeper. Our people don't come to Mass to be entertained. They can find that elsewhere. The real problem is not that they are bored—but that they are disappointed. Why? Because in the Mass they do not experience *contact with God*. They do not feel touched by God. And *that* is what they are hoping for when they come to worship. They know that the Mass is not supposed to be entertainment. It is prayer. And they are disappointed because too often they experience it not as prayer but as ritual—

going through the motions without heart or soul. So they do not feel touched by God (pp. 77-82).

If this analysis is accurate, then the question emerges: What can we do to make the Sunday Eucharist more prayerful, and therefore more evangelizing? Granted, contact with God cannot be manipulated; it is God's free gift. But how can we create the sacred environment that will enable people to open themselves to the experience of God? Here's where our pastoral liturgists and musicians can contribute their expertise. For one thing, good music is a powerful means of evangelization. Whenever I ask people what they appreciate about liturgy in their parish, music always ranks near the top. Music that is relatively easy to sing, words that speak of the mystery of God and God's compassion for our human struggles, the dying and rising of Jesus, our hope for eternal life—these are what nourish people's faith. The words and melodies often linger with them long after the Mass is ended. Moreover, if the parish has good cantors and a choir that truly prays the music as well as they sing it, people are touched at a deep level of spirit. If you have any doubts about the power of music to move the soul, think of the throngs that spend forty to fifty dollars to attend a pop concert.

As leader of prayer, the priest who presides at the liturgy has a crucial role in creating the sacred atmosphere. Does he truly proclaim the gospel passage, not just read it? Does he *pray* (not merely recite or rush through) those great eucharistic prayers that remind us of all that God has done for us in Jesus Christ? Do he and the other eucharistic ministers distribute the consecrated bread and wine with a deep sense of faith in the Real Presence of Christ? Are there periods of silence after the homily and after Communion, wherein people can savor Christ's presence in both word and sacrament? It is often said—and bears repeating—that the Sunday Eucharist is the primary means of evangelization for the gathered community of active Catholics. As we will see, it is often also a potentially evangelizing moment for inactive Catholics and unchurched people who may be in attendance.

Growth in Faith

Besides the Sunday Eucharist, what are some other ways of "creating enthusiasm for their faith among active Catholics" (Goal I of the bishops' Pastoral Plan)? The bishops mention fostering "a renewed understanding of the Faith." Since many Catholics are notoriously deficient in an adult understanding of their faith, the bishops see the need for quality adult education programs in the parishes. Among other things, the publication of the new *Catechism of the Catholic Church* offers a timely opportunity to invite parishioners to come together for a deeper study of their faith. However, as every parish knows, even the best designed adult formation programs featuring the finest presenters typically fail to attract more than a handful of parishioners. As I mentioned before, I am puzzled by the fact that the same people who eagerly attend workshops to update their knowledge and skills for their secular profession will often do little to grow in their religious knowledge. Could the reason be that there is no financial incentive? Still, I believe parishes must continue to offer and promote quality adult education opportunities. An excellent resource is the U.S. bishops' pastoral plan for adult faith formation: *Our Hearts Were Burning Within Us* (USCC, 1999).

The same holds true for spiritual renewal programs. With all its defects, the church of the 1960s and 70s developed several forms of what I call "foundational experiences." Programs like the Cursillo, Marriage Encounter, and the Christian Family Movement produced a couple generations of lay people who were deeply grounded in spirituality and often emerged as leaders in their parishes. For reasons I don't understand, these movements have diminished considerably. I find myself asking, "Where do people find their 'foundational experiences' of conversion and spiritual awakening today?" Perhaps in the programs of lay leadership formation that now exist in a number of dioceses. But these are limited to small numbers of people who can commit several years of weekend study for this purpose. I am convinced that we must provide opportunities for ordinary people to grow beyond being Sunday-only Catholics to become deeply committed and enthusiastic believers. These are the people who will become the lay evangelizers of the future. In my work at the retreat center, I often observe people who undergo a profound spiritual awakening at the weekend retreat. I wish there were some way that that energy could be channeled when they return to their parishes. One of my dreams is that a parish or parish cluster will commit to a retreat weekend open to the whole parish, where a significant group of parishioners will have a common "foundational experience" of Christ's presence and love, of the meaning of their baptism, and of their call to evangelize. This model already exists in the program "Christ Renews His Parish," but I believe it could be replicated in other forms.

On a smaller scale, many parishes are helping to nurture people's faith through the experience of Bible study. There are a number of outstanding packaged programs to aid in this endeavor, while other parishes rely on trained local facilitators. The strength of such programs is that people not only learn more about scripture, but also have an opportunity to connect the word of God with their own lives and to share their insights and experiences with one another. This serves to strengthen and support everyone in their faith journey. Here the example of the Latin American "base communities" readily comes to mind. Shortly after

Vatican II, many bishops, priests, and other church leaders recognized that the faith of the people could no longer be maintained by the usual pastoral methods—baptism, minimal preparation for the other sacraments, a visit from an itinerant priest every three to six months. So they began forming local catechists and lay leaders in the study of scripture and its applications to the daily lives of the people. These leaders were then empowered and commissioned to conduct Bible reflection and faith sharing in small groups in the villages and rural areas where priests and sisters were not readily available. People not only became enthused about their faith, but also bonded together as supportive Christian communities. Moreover, they became aware that the gospel sometimes called them to work together to change social conditions that were depriving them of their basic rights and of access to the resources of God's creation. This model of faith sharing has been adapted for parish communities also in North America. Indeed, many Catholics have found their "foundational experiences" or at least a strong awakening of faith through these small group gatherings.

Other parishes are helping to nurture faith by offering teachings and experiences of prayer. The bishops' Pastoral Plan mentions a number of possibilities: scheduling the Liturgy of the Hours or other forms of communal prayer as a regular part of parish life; offering forms of popular devotion, whether old or new; encouraging the formation of prayer groups; teaching various methods of prayer, such as meditation and contemplation; making good spiritual reading available.

The intent of Goal I is clear: We need to be joyful, loving, faith-filled people if we are going to try to evangelize others. The bishops are calling each of us and our parish communities to lifelong conversion and growth in our relationship with Jesus Christ. That is the only solid basis for reaching out to "the ungathered" and sharing with them the spiritual treasure we have found.

Training for One-to-One Evangelizing

One very direct way to create enthusiasm for the faith among active parishioners is to offer a training course in one-to-one evangelization. I often call this "kitchen table" or "workplace" evangelizing, and I have conducted the course in a number of parishes. It appeals to many people because it doesn't require them to do public speaking or to memorize a set of Bible texts. I have taken the main outline of the course from Susan Blum's booklet *The Ministry of Evangelization* (Liturgical Press, 1988), and adapted it for my own purposes.

Ideally, the course consists of four two-hour sessions held once a week. I begin by presenting the New Testament foundations for evangelization, using the gospels and Acts of the Apostles. I then give a brief history of evangelization in the United States, showing why we as Catholics have been reluctant to evangelize and why the call is urgent at the present time. I follow with a brief summary of Pope Paul VI's document on evangelization and the U.S. Bishops' Pastoral Plan. Then I explain what evangelization is and is not, much as I did in Chapter 3. Most of the remainder of the course is devoted to explaining and practicing a five-step process for evangelizing individuals who may be searching for something to believe in ("seekers").

1. *Listening.* Participants are often surprised to hear that evangelizing begins with listening rather than talking. I invite them to imagine various scenarios wherein people begin talking with them about their concerns: in the doctor's office where someone confides in them a worry about health problems; a parent upset about their son or daughter's behavior; a spouse troubled by tensions in their marriage, perhaps even discovery of

their spouse involved in an affair; someone worried by rumors of downsizing in the company and possible layoffs; someone grieving the loss of a loved one; a teen feeling left out of the peer group or being dumped by a boyfriend or girlfriend. Instead of giving out some easy advice or pious cliché, the evangelizers are asked to listen carefully and respond in an empathic, non-judgmental manner. Perhaps they will ask a few questions to clarify the situation, so that the person feels understood and accepted.

2. *Sharing Your Story*. I go on to tell the participants: At some point, when you sense it is the right moment, you say something like: "You know, I've gone through something like that in my own life. And what helped me most was my faith in God." Then you go on to share briefly what happened. So now you have moved the conversation to the spiritual level. As I've said before, we Catholics do not readily talk about our faith. Somehow we got the idea that religion is a very private matter best kept to oneself. But we are not alone in this. George Gallup, who has been taking the religious pulse of Americans for decades, says that his surveys show that nearly 75% of the United States population claims to have had life-changing spiritual experiences. That is an awesome statistic. But even more surprising: most people do not talk about these experiences. That tells us at least two things: 1) God is still very active in the lives of people; and 2) most of us have spiritual "stories" to share—stories that could inspire others to search for God. Think about it: Where have you found God in your life?

🕊 Was it when you were praying about some anxiety, and you felt a great peace come over you, like God was saying, "Don't worry; it's going to be OK"?

🕊 Was it when you read the Bible or heard a homily, and suddenly you knew that you were held in God's love and that Jesus was truly your friend?

🍃 Was it after that stormy period in your life when you looked back and said, "How did we ever get through that? I know God was with us"?

🍃 Was it when you held your newborn baby in your arms, were in awe at the mystery of life, and knew that only God could make such a perfect little creature?

🍃 Was it when you beheld a magnificent sunrise or sunset, or stood in awe at the vast ocean in front of you, or gazed intently at that delicate, beautiful flower at your feet—and felt wrapped in wonder at the creative power of God?

🍃 Was it when your teenager, who hadn't done a lick of work around the house in light years, suddenly said, "Looks like you and Dad need a break; I'll clean the house this weekend"?

Whatever it was, you simply share the story of how God helped you through a difficult time in your life. The beauty of this approach is its simplicity and non-intrusiveness. You do not argue; you do not boast; you do not "talk theology." You simply share your own experience. When finished, you give the other person a chance to respond. Perhaps this is as far as they are willing to go at this point, which is fine. They have had a good experience of being listened to and understood. You have given them something to think about. You can promise to pray for them, invite them to talk again, exchange phone numbers. In any case, it is a grace moment.

3. *Sharing the Gospel.* With some seekers, however, you may be able to move further. They may say something like: "Tell me more about what you believe." Or, "That's fine for you, but how do I know God is there for me?" So you may want to take another step in the evangelizing process: sharing something of the gospel

of Jesus. After all, we want to lead people to him, not to ourselves. So you share with the seeker one of your favorite gospel stories or teachings. For instance, with someone who has wandered away from God or church for a long time, you might tell (in your own words) the story of the Prodigal Son (or better, the wayward son and the forgiving father). With someone battling illness, you may share one of Jesus' healing miracles. With someone grieving a lost loved one, you may recall how Jesus himself wept over the death of his friend Lazarus and assured his sisters that he (and all of us) will be raised to fullness of life with God and with one another. You may also use examples from the Old Testament. As I mentioned before, you don't need to have biblical quotes memorized. We can simply summarize or tell the story in our own words. When we have taken the time to listen to the other's pain, and when we share the scriptures from our own hearts, wonderful things can happen. It is like a sacramental moment.

4. *Invitation.* If the seeker is still engaged and appears to be open, we may take yet another evangelizing step. We may invite them to make one small move, whatever they are ready for, toward God or toward reconnecting with the church community. As a most basic step, we can invite them to begin praying— for guidance, for strength, for healing. If they are Catholics who have stopped practicing, we can ask what happened, how they drifted away. Once we have heard their story, we can gently invite them "to take another look," as the Paulists like to say. We may tell them about a course on Catholicism or on the Bible being offered at our parish, or to an inquiry class, or to a Christian music concert. If they seem ready, we can invite them to attend Sunday Mass. In all these cases, it is best if we offer to accompany them and introduce them to people; most seekers are reluctant to take those

steps on their own. If they are in a second marriage, we may offer to introduce them to the pastor to see if their marriage can be blessed in the church and they can return to the sacraments. In any case, what have you lost by extending an invitation? The most the person can do is turn it down. On the other hand, a good deal of recent research has shown that many inactive Catholics are not happy about being disconnected. But they are too embarrassed, or don't know how, to reconnect. If someone from the church reaches out a hand, they will take it. Of course, if your parish is lifeless or riddled with conflict, don't bother inviting! But perhaps you can direct them to a life-giving parish elsewhere.

5. *Integration Into Community.* This is the final step in the evangelizing process. Some of the points mentioned above are already part of this. Interestingly, I read one piece of research that found that new members or returning members of a church tend not to remain unless they form relational bonds with at least seven members of the church community. This is eloquent testimony to the crucial importance of communal support for our faith. Returning Catholics will cover quite a spectrum here. Some need only to make a good confession and resume Mass attendance. Others will simply need some encouragement and support from welcoming parishioners. Some have been poorly instructed or have lost touch with Catholic teachings, so they will need something like the RCIA process for re-entry. Others have been hurt by church people, so they will need an experience of being listened to, perhaps offered an apology, and some honest gestures of healing and reconciliation. For inactive Protestants and other unchurched persons, the RCIA will be the ideal process for integration into the community.

After I present this model of one-to-one evangelization, we spend time practicing the skills of listening, sharing our stories, sharing the gospel, and inviting. We role play various types of seekers, observe how the would-be evangelizer responds, and give constructive feedback. What typically happens is that participants begin to develop a sense of confidence: "Yes, I think I can do this. It's not so complicated." In the weeks between classes I encourage them to: 1) pray for the grace to be a good evangelizer; 2) watch for opportunities to listen and evangelize one-on-one. I begin each class by asking: "How did you evangelize or how were you evangelized this week?" It is always inspiring to hear what comes forth, how participants begin to notice evangelizing moments in their lives that would have escaped them before.

In the final class, we consider some common objections the participants may encounter: e.g., why do we need a church? why do we need confession to a priest? why do Catholics "worship" Mary and the saints? The immediate benefit of this course is that it equips a group of lay people in the parish with the knowledge and skills to reach out to that large group of inactive Catholics and unchurched persons whom they encounter in the workplace, at sporting events and concerts, at the beauty shop or barber shop, or right in their own families. Whenever possible, I try to gather "the graduates" together for a follow-up or refresher session wherein they can share their successes and difficulties in evangelizing, ask questions, and so on. One of the needs I am discovering is for the participants to have some basic grounding in "apologetics"—the knowledge and ability to give reasonable explanations of certain "sticking" points of Catholic doctrine: the Bible as sole authority for belief; salvation by faith or by good works; papal authority; creation and evolution; sexual morality. (I will discuss some of these issues more at length in the last chapter of this book.) Finally, I am convinced of the need to train other lay people to conduct the course on their own.

Evangelizing
Inactive
Catholics
and the
Unchurched

Important as it is, the church's evangelizing ministry does not begin and end with active, church-going parishioners. I mentioned before that the typical parish has often settled into a static, "maintenance" mode of operating, rather than a dynamic, mission-driven mode. "We take care of our own" is not an adequate mission statement for a parish community. Parishes today are invited to see themselves as responsible for the spiritual welfare of all the people in their territory. That is a visionary and inclusive ecclesiology. "Cast your nets wide!" it seems to be saying. What if we took it seriously? It would propel us outward, directing our ministry not only to those in the pews but also to those "on the margin," those we are not reaching by our usual pastoral programs and services. The purpose of nourishing and strengthening the faith of our active Catholics is not only to support them spiritually but also to empower them to spread the gospel more effectively.

For various reasons, our Catholic people do not readily think of themselves as evangelizers. I have often regretted that the Roman Missal translates the Latin dismissal (*Ite, missa est*) as "The Mass is ended, go in peace." The English sounds too much like, "That's all, folks; go home in comfort." The Latin is really saying, "Go, you are sent forth!" *Missa est* means "You have a mission." The Mass is the greatest act of prayer and worship imaginable. It nourishes and strengthens our faith. But it also sends us out, gives us a mission. The "gathered" community moves out to the "ungathered" with the good news that Jesus came to bring: "God is here for you!" So the second goal of the U.S. Bishops' plan *Go and Make Disciples* is to invite all people, in particular the unchurched, to hear the church's message of salvation so that all may unite in Jesus Christ.

Outreach to Inactive Catholics

In the first pages of this book I noted the research showing the huge number of baptized but non-practicing Catholics, usually referred to as "inactive." As a descriptive word, however, it may be misleading. Such Catholics may be "active" in practicing their faith in many ways: living good ethical/moral lives, praying, reading scripture and other spiritual books, being involved in caring for the poor and neglected members of society, perhaps even making retreats. What separates active from inactive Catholics, in George Gallup's surveys, is church attendance. One can easily find fault with such a definition. For it ignores the fact that many church attendees may be far less "active," in terms of practical Christianity, than many who do not attend church.

Nevertheless, there is no question that vast numbers of Catholics have given up their visible connection with the church. Every time I address a parish group about this issue, I ask how many people there have at least one relative or friend who has dropped out of church attendance. Invariably, practically every hand goes up (including my own). For years I wondered why no one seemed to be speaking or writing about this phenomenon. In recent years, however, there has been an outpouring of concern. In 1999 the Evangelization Committee of the National Conference of Catholic Bishops published an outstanding booklet entitled *A Time to Listen . . . A Time to Heal: A Resource Directory for Reaching Out to Inactive Catholics*. The first article is a fine piece by Paulist Fr. Frank DeSiano: "It Is Mercy I Want." He grounds the outreach to inactive Catholics in the gospels, particularly Jesus' own concern for the lost and marginalized people of his time, and the commission he gave the church to be a community of reconciliation. "Catholic after Catholic," he says, "want our parishes to reach out to these brothers and sisters who are no longer connected to their faith community." He says Catholics can understand this call for reconciliation because they know so many in that situation:

𝖜 Their own children and grandchildren, plus neighbors, who just drifted away from the practice of the faith as part of their "growing up";

𝖜 Sons and daughters who married with great hopes, only to have those hopes dashed by marital conflict and divorce, who now feel excluded from the table of Christ;

𝖜 Family members who were raised as solid Catholics, but felt unable to accept some of the changes in the church, or were disillusioned by the lack of change;

𝖜 Friends and family members who have joined another church and are now challenging them about the defects in their Catholic beliefs and practices;

𝖜 Someone who was hurt or offended by someone in the church, and walked away in sadness or disgust.

The need for a ministry of reconciliation and healing is beyond question.

Methods of Outreach

For a long time, it seemed, individuals and parishes were feeling the need for such a ministry but were unclear as to how to go about it. They instinctively recoiled from any kind of approach based on guilt or shame. But in recent years the Holy Spirit has been stirring up a good number of people to develop creative and gospel-based forms of outreach. The resource from the Bishops' Committee noted above gives an excellent summary of the various approaches. Some are parish-based; others are diocesan and even nationwide in scope. The basic message we want to communicate to our inactive brothers and sisters is this: "We miss you. We care about you. We invite you to take another look at our community. You will be welcome here."

Let me now try to describe the various elements that would comprise an effective parish-based ministry to inactive Catholics.

1. *Total Parish Involvement.* It may seem obvious, but this needs to be stated: The ministry is doomed to failure if it does not have the wholehearted support of the pastor. Sometimes I get calls from parishioners who have caught the fire and want me to help them get started with an outreach to inactive Catholics. But I will not do so if the pastor is not on board. My practice is not based on ideological grounds but on practical ones: the parish simply will not follow unless the pastor leads. In fact, the whole pastoral team or staff needs to support the ministry. Nor is it enough that an Evangelization Committee be given the task. It is *the whole parish* that is the agent of evangelization. The committee, or the pastoral staff, may do the visioning and planning and actual carrying out of the ministry.

But the whole parish needs to be informed and involved. In reality, this is not very difficult. If the pastor and staff begin to inform parish members—through homilies, bulletin announcements, and the like—that the parish is planning to reach out to inactive Catholics in their midst, parishioners will be both grateful and supportive. They will gladly pray for God's blessing on the ministry, because they hope it will reach their own inactive loved ones. By all means, homebound members and nursing home residents should be asked for their prayerful support.

2. *Simple, Basic Ways.* I will never forget what I once heard a businessman say to me: "You priests have the greatest product in the world (meaning the gospel), but you don't know how to market it." Perhaps we resist "marketplace" language when thinking of spreading the gospel—but why not? As St. Paul once said: "How can they call on [God] in whom they have not believed? And how can they believe in him of whom they have not heard? And how can they hear without someone to preach?" (Rom 10:14). Marketing is simply a way of getting the gospel message out into the public arena. More specifically, it is letting people know that our parish is here, it has something good to offer, and you will be welcome. Here are some suggestions I never tire of presenting to parishes:

🕊 Create an attractive, welcoming physical environment. This includes a clear, easily readable sign for the parish office. I don't know how many times I have had to drive up and down streets and through parking lots in search of some clue as to "Where the heck is the entrance?" It should not be that difficult to design signs and access to our places with "spiritual seekers" in mind. Make it as easy as possible. Signs outside the church are helpful to announce the times of services. But they could also include a friendly message such as "All Visitors Welcome"; or

"God's Family Includes You." Speaking of welcome, one of the key persons in the parish is surely the secretary-receptionist. Hers is usually the first voice or face the visitor will encounter. Is it warm and welcoming, or cold and indifferent? I have experienced all kinds, for the most part on the positive side. But there have been some painful exceptions. Just recently a parent told me her college-age daughter has a friend who wanted to become Catholic. She called five different churches in one city to ask about joining. Four of them never returned her call. At the fifth, the secretary insisted on knowing the reason why she wanted to become Catholic! Wouldn't it have been much simpler (and more Christlike) if she had been told: "I'm so glad you're thinking of joining us. The pastor would like to meet with you to talk about the process. He has openings—when could you come?" Evangelization takes place so often in ordinary moments such as this.

❧ I have also been encouraging parishes to create a simple but attractive parish brochure or flyer. I have collected a number of these over the years. Most are just folded paper with some pictures (photos or drawings) and basic information about parish services, phone numbers, etc. Nearly every parish has someone gifted in graphic arts or computer layout who could help design such a flyer. After copies or prints are made, they are given to parishioners to hand out to friends, leave in workplaces or public transits, waiting rooms, and so on. The purpose is to create awareness of the parish—its name, location, and available services. Similarly, an attractive poster can be designed to display in offices or business places of parishioners. Make sure everyone in the community knows there is a St. Michael's or St. Rita's parish where they will find welcome.

❧ Sometimes, when inactive Catholics find the courage to attend Mass or some other church service, they are either gratified or turned off by the kind of reception they experience. Here is where people who serve as greeters or ministers of hospitality have an important role. Without being gushy, they can communicate a genuine sense of warmth and welcome. But the burden should not be all on the greeters. Again, this is a total parish endeavor. Do the other parishioners smile, scowl, or ignore the newcomer? Do they refuse to give them a place in their pew? If the newcomer is fumbling for the right hymn, will anyone help? Not long ago I attended Sunday Mass while on vacation. The commentator began, in a friendly way, by welcoming everyone to the service. Then he asked, "If there are any visitors here, would you please stand up?" A few of us did. Immediately a greeter or usher came over and handed us a "Visitor Card." It had a warm message like: *Thank you for worshipping with us. Would you like to know more about our parish? Please fill out this card, return it to one of the Hospitality Ministers or the collection basket, and we will be happy to contact you.* At the bottom it said: "Come as a guest; leave as a friend." I remember saying to myself: "If I were looking for a parish community, I would fill out that card and turn it in." A couple of cautions. For one, some people are embarrassed to stand up and be seen as visitors; maybe it would be better to call attention to the cards and just invite visitors to take one and fill it out. For another, it is crucial that somebody from the parish follow up with a phone call or visit as soon as possible. Nothing is so disheartening as taking the risk to hand in your name and number, and then being forgotten. That may be the last gesture an inactive Catholic will ever attempt.

❦ Another simple form of outreach: in our highly mobile society, people are forever moving in and out of parish boundaries and neighborhoods. I'm told it's not too difficult for the parish to stay informed (through realtors and others) about newcomers moving in. Chances are great that some of them will be marginal Catholics or unchurched people. Why not train a small core of parishioners to make a call or (better yet) pay a personal visit to each newcomer? With a plate of cookies and a parish brochure, welcome them into the neighborhood and tell them about the parish. It is well known that many people (not only Catholics) drop out of church after moving to a new location. Often it's not rejection but a simple matter of inertia: "We got preoccupied with our house and yard, finding a school, doctors and dentists, health club, etc. Just never got around to connecting with a church." Personal contact with a friendly parishioner may be all the nudge they need.

❦ If at all possible, create a Web site for your parish. Again, a lot of inactive and unchurched people do their spiritual seeking via the Internet. I have seen some wonderful parish web sites that include not only basic information but attractive pictures, announcements, brief meditations, inspiring stories or anecdotes, names and phone numbers of key people and services. Be sure to include a friendly message to spiritual seekers and provide an e-mail address where they can ask questions and engage in dialogue. I'm convinced that if St. Paul were alive today, he'd be all over the Internet.

❦ One more simple suggestion. Christmas and Easter are privileged moments of grace for many inactive Catholics. Your parish might want to send out a bulk mailing to every address in your zip code with a message: *If you have no place to worship this holiday, you would be most welcome to join us.* Then list your address and phone, times of services, and a special spiritual message from the pastor. Or, if your holiday Masses are already overcrowded, you can at least extend a warm welcome to all guests and newcomers, invite them to come again and to take a parish bulletin with them. It may just be the bit of encouragement they need to reconnect with the church of their baptism.

3. *More Concentrated Ways.* Every parish, I presume, has a roster or membership list of its parishioners. Pastors sometimes speak of "dead wood" on their rosters, meaning people who no longer appear in church or at least do not turn in weekly parish envelopes. This is a natural "target group" for outreach. Someone on the parish staff, or one or more trained lay persons, could make a phone call or a home visit to these parishioners. The message is not, "Why haven't you been supporting the parish?" but, "We've missed seeing you. How are you doing? Is there a reason you haven't been joining us for worship?" The purpose is not to induce guilt but to express concern. About a year ago Bishop Michael Saltarelli of Wilmington, Delaware wrote a beautiful pastoral letter on "How to Reach Inactive Catholics" (See *Origins*, Jan. 27, 2000, pp. 514-18). In it he quoted Paulist Fr. John Hurley who said, "Many [Catholics] drop away with the hope that someone will notice; and with large congregations in many parishes, often no one does. Would you want to join a church that doesn't care when you fall away?" Good question. In some cases, of course, the people have simply moved away or joined another parish. But if they are staying away because of an invalid marriage, or are feeling hurt or disappointed with the parish, or are preoccupied with a family problem, pastors would want to know. It could lead to a process of healing and reconciliation.

An even more ambitious form of outreach would be a phone call or personal visit to everyone on the parish roster. This is akin to what was formerly called "the parish census." It requires a great deal of time and planning, but the rewards can be substantial. The parish would almost certainly have to train some lay members for this ministry. The purpose would have to be clarified and understood by both callers and parishioners. It is not merely to collect data (how many children, which sacraments received, etc.), but a truly pastoral call. Invitation-type questions such as: How is your life going? What do you find helpful in the parish? How could the parish serve you better? How would you like to be involved in the parish's ministries? Would you like to talk to one of the priests or parish staff? Such inquiries can produce a wealth of important data. But callers or visitors would have to be cautioned not to get into arguments or become defensive about the parish. They are there to listen and try to understand without judging. Moreover, some kind of follow-up will often be necessary. It can be devastating for people to open up some painful area of their life, agree to discuss it further—and then receive no response. Another problem: it is difficult to find people at home, except during some evening and weekend hours. Or, if they are home, they do not answer the phone or doorbell. So it is crucial to announce to the parishioners that during such-and-such a time period they can expect a call or visit from parish people for the purpose of getting a clearer picture of the parish and its needs. Incidentally, if a personal visit is the method of choice, it is better to have the visitors go in pairs. Besides providing mutual support, they can alternate taking the lead in the interviews. In any case, such a call or visit will invariably turn up a significant number of inactive Catholics. Imagine the opportunities for healing and reconciliation.

"Welcome Home" Programs

In the past ten years or so, a good number of parishes, as well as dioceses, have developed a form of outreach to inactive Catholics, variously named "Welcome Home," "Catholics Returning," and the like. These are generally focused, time-limited programs offered two or three times a year at a given parish or parish cluster. Again, it is crucial that the entire parish be informed and involved in this ministry. Besides being spoken of from the pulpit and announced in the bulletin, usually a letter is sent to all on the parish roster (see sample letter in Appendix, pp. 185-186). Typically, the letter asks active parishioners to personally invite their inactive Catholic family members, friends, co-workers, etc. to attend a "listening session" on a specified day or evening, and to offer to accompany the person (since many inactive Catholics are reluctant to attend a church event alone). The session is billed as an opportunity for inactive Catholics to share their concerns or problems with the church, to ask questions in the presence of the pastor and a few parishioners who will listen to them in an open, caring manner. It is stressed that there will be no fees and no obligation to rejoin the parish. The sole purpose is to hear the stories and the questions. The letter also states that if the reader is an inactive Catholic, he or she is specially invited to attend the session. In addition, the listening session is announced at Masses and in the bulletin as well as in other media (newspaper or local community paper, radio spots, posters, etc.).

A key component of this ministry is a carefully selected and trained "listening team." Members may be chosen from the parish Evangelization Committee, if one exists, and possibly some others. At least one (preferably two) of the team should be formerly inactive Catholics who have returned. There has been some discussion as to whether the pastor ought to be part of the team. Some think not, lest his presence inhibit the inactive Catholics from freely expressing their feelings. I personally believe that the pastor—or at least someone from the pastoral staff who represents "the official church"—should be present. Otherwise people can say, "Why isn't the priest here? He needs to hear some of these things." At the very least, the pastor should be present at one or more of the later sessions. All team members should be people who are friendly and welcoming; be able to listen to the inactive Catholics without the need to defend the church or try to "fix" anything; be committed to the church, even if they have some problems with it; and have a sense of humor. One of the team members acts as facilitator. It is important that he or she set a tone of welcome and openness and be able to elicit the concerns of the group.

I have facilitated these listening sessions in a number of different parishes and clusters. Inactive Catholics have numbered from four to twenty-two. With some modifications, I basically follow the model described in *Catholics Coming Home*, by Carrie Kemp and Donald Pologruto (HarperCollins, 1990). I have always found it to be a richly rewarding experience. After setting the tone and assuring confidentiality, I note that each of us here is on a spiritual journey, and we want to honor that journey. I then ask the team members who became inactive and then returned to share their story; this in itself can be a moving experience. Then I invite the inactive "guests" to share their experiences of church. They begin hesitantly, but before long there is an outpouring of pain, disappointment, and anger, mixed in with positive memories and humorous stories. At the end, I invite the participants to stay for a social (coffee and cookies) and a chance to talk to team members one-to-one.

I have found the experience to be consistently positive. Participants usually leave with a feeling of being heard and respected, even though their problems and questions may not have been resolved. They see clearly that they are not alone, that others have had similar hurtful experiences with the church, but that doors are open for healing and reconciliation. The hardest part is knowing what to do by way of follow-up. The listening session is a good beginning, but the process needs to continue. So we tell the participants we plan to schedule three more weekly sessions wherein we can address the concerns that surfaced tonight. We ask them, toward the end of the listening session, to write on cards the questions or issues they would like to have discussed in subsequent sessions. After reading them aloud, we agree on a topic for the next week and invite everyone to return. Later, the team goes over the other cards and decides how to address them in the final two sessions. This is not a bad plan; the problem is, while most return for the second session, hardly anyone comes for the last two. Fortunately, by the end of the second session most participants have connected personally with one of the team members, who then tries to stay in touch with them on their spiritual journey.

Lately I have noticed that a number of parishes state, in their initial announcements, that the "Coming Home" program will run for three or even up to six sessions. Sometimes titles are given for each session, usually covering such topics as divorce/annulments, changes in the church, understanding the Bible, an explanation of the Mass, confession, ways of prayer. That way, individuals can choose to attend the sessions they feel they need. It should be noted that some inactive Catholics, while baptized, may be so deficient in knowledge of their faith that they could be placed in an RCIA process.

In any case, I regard this kind of outreach as practically a "no-fail" ministry. As we noted before, many inactive Catholics are looking for signs that they would be welcomed back in the church if they were ready. They will usually not take the initiative, but if they hear of an invitation to attend a no obligation event, they may take the risk. Which is why, for the most part, some people will always show up for a listening session (or however it is billed). They may not be ready for a full return, but if they have a reasonably good experience, the seed has been dropped into the tilled soil. And the cost to the parish has been minimal. Even if only one person has been touched by God's grace through this process, it has been worth it. Moreover, even if no one actually returns to the church, "the word is out" that your parish or district really cares about alienated, hurting Catholics and is willing to reach out to them. I recall when I was working with a group of three parishes for this ministry, the local newspaper heard about it and did a lengthy front page story for its Sunday edition. The parishes couldn't have gotten better publicity if they had paid for it. I find it both sad and amusing that "Catholics evangelizing" makes the daily news.

Outreach to Unchurched People

Evangelization is not limited to Catholics, whether active or inactive. It also extends to those who do not believe in Jesus Christ or, if they do, are not connected to any church community. George Gallup estimates there are about 80 million of these in the United States, a remarkably high number considering this country is usually regarded as a "Christian" nation. Gallup calls this phenomenon "believing without belonging." Sociologists would say that this reflects the typically American preference for individual freedom as opposed to group adherence. "Religion is a purely private matter" is the unquestioned belief of many. Which is why a majority (perhaps) of the unchurched would fall into the category of "satisfied" (as I described earlier) rather than "seekers." They do not feel the need to belong to a spiritual community. On the other hand, there have always been people who come to feel that "going it alone" is not working for them. But that feeling may be muffled under many layers of prejudices against churchgoing people or fear of losing one's independence.

Whatever the underlying dynamics, there are clearly a good number of unchurched people who would be open to the gospel of Christ and to the Christian community. And the church recognizes its call to evangelize all types of people. Pope Paul VI spoke of the need to offer the gospel both to unbelievers and to those who have been baptized but have never lived it or even been instructed in the basics of Christianity:

> Atheistic secularism and the absence of religious practice are found among adults and among the young . . . at all levels of education, and in both the old churches and the young ones. The Church's evangelizing action cannot ignore these two worlds . . . it must constantly seek the proper means and language for presenting, or re-presenting, to them God's revelation and faith in Jesus Christ (*On Evangelization in the Modern World*, n. 56).

But the question remains: What could be some forms of outreach to the unchurched? Until recently I was pretty well convinced that this could be done only through one-to-one evangelizing. In my training course for that ministry, I encourage participants not to be put off by people who "don't believe in going to church," but to engage them in dialogue. Sometimes I role play people who say: "I don't need a church; I can pray to God at home—or in the woods." Or: "I was baptized Protestant, but our family never went to church." Such people may indeed be among "the satisfied" who are not interested in moving any further; but they may also be "seekers" who are open. So I coach the evangelizers to ask a question like, "Do you ever wish you were part of a church community—or wonder what it would be like?" If they say yes, invite them to keep talking. If no, you can still "drop a few seeds" by sharing your own experience: "I'm glad you believe in God and are trying to walk a spiritual path. But for me, I've found that I need help in keeping God in the center of my life. Otherwise I can too easily get lost in all the other stuff coming at me all day. So I need a church, a community of people to help me stay close to God. And I'm happy to say that at our church we have a very warm, caring community of people. Would you like to come with me some time to see for yourself?"

I still believe this is a graceful and effective way to evangelize the unchurched. But I've learned that sometimes the "Welcome Home" programs I described will attract unchurched people as well as inactive Catholics. This is particularly true when the invitation has been broadened along the lines of: "If you would like to learn more about the Catholic Church, come and join us for. . . ." Some unchurched people, baptized or not, are sometimes inexplicably drawn to the Catholic Church and might feel safe in becoming part of a group of learners.

Let me suggest yet another initiative for reaching the unchurched: a door-to-door visitation of every residence in a given geographic area. This is a daunting task which requires a great deal of planning and work on the part of the parish. For this reason, it is wise to think about collaborating with one or more parishes in the area. Once again, it is crucial to inform the whole parish about the project and to request their prayer support. Some of the more important steps would be:

🌿 Informing the Protestant, Jewish, and Muslim communities in the area that such a visitation will be taking place and assuring them that there will be no proselytizing or attempts to lure away their practicing members.

🌿 Sending a letter to every residence of the area to be visited, explaining the purpose of the visit and asking for their cooperation. A sample of such a letter can be found in the Appendix, pages 186-187.

⚜ Recruiting and training a sufficient number of visitors. This can be a delicate process. If you open it up to anyone interested, you may end up with some people who are not suited: they may be overbearing, too eager to "make converts," prone to getting embroiled in arguments, and so forth. On the other hand, if you hand pick the visitors, there may be resentment on the part of some who are passed over. Also, because people are so busy, it may be difficult to recruit enough visitors to make the task manageable. The training need not be extensive: some basic skills in asking questions and listening well; communicating a sincere interest in the people and their life concerns; some brief witnessing of how the visitors' faith and membership in the parish have helped them.

⚜ Some form of record-keeping and planning for follow-up. Visitors will need to make notes about their visits, particularly with those who show some interest in connecting or reconnecting with the parish, or Catholics with children who have not received some sacraments or are in need of catechesis. These notations are best made immediately after the visit. This is usually more effective if the visitors go out in pairs, since one may recall some things that the other missed.

Admittedly, there are notable difficulties in this large-scale kind of outreach. At the same time, the payoffs can be significant. Such a visitation will identify many inactive Catholics as well as unchurched people with no religious affiliation. Moreover, it lends itself to media coverage and places the parish(es) squarely in the public eye. And it will be a clear sign to the active parishioners that they are becoming a mission-driven, evangelizing parish. Just last month I talked to a pastor who is planning an ecumenical door-to-door visitation in cooperation with all seven Christian churches in the area. It appears to be well planned, and I look forward to hearing about the results.

One more recent development has come from the Episcopal Church in England and made its way into the United States. It is a program called "Alpha," and is designed specifically as an outreach to unchurched people. But its promotional material states that it is intended for anyone who is interested in: the existence of God; the purpose of life; what happens after death; who Jesus Christ is and what he taught; the nature and purpose of the church; sin and forgiveness; moral questions. In a word, it is a course in Christianity 101. The course begins with a simple evening meal followed by a video presentation and small-group discussion. The course then continues for ten more weeks. The video presentations are by the Rev. Nicky Gumbel, an Anglican priest with an engaging and humorous manner. The videos show large crowds with mostly young people in attendance. One gets the impression that the course is reaching those many "Generation X and Y" people who grew up with little or no Christian formation. The blurbs claim that more than a million people around the world have completed the Alpha course. (The U.S. office can be reached at 1-888-949-2574; e-mail: alphana@aol.com.)

I am in no position to pass judgment on the course, since I've only seen the introductory video. But I know it has received a positive endorsement from several Catholic dioceses in the U.S. as well as in the United Kingdom. The fact that Alpha attracts sizable crowds is a clear indicator that a lot of unchurched people are indeed searching for something to believe in amid a secularized world. There is also a program called "Alpha for Catholics." Basically, it encourages parishes to make use of the Alpha course, but to supplement it with a set of videos that present specific aspects of Catholic teaching, especially the sacraments. Alpha for

Catholics is sponsored by CHRISTLIFE (1-888-498-8474; www.christlife.org).

Our Inactive and Unchurched Children

Whenever I give talks to parish groups about reaching out to inactive Catholics and unchurched people, parents (and grandparents) in the audience inevitably ask: "What about our own adult children who have left the church?" Then come the expressions of pain and grief: We tried so hard to bring them up in the Faith. We sent them to Catholic schools, made sure they went to church and received all the sacraments. But when they left home or got married, they dropped it all. Their own children aren't getting any religious upbringing—aren't even baptized or haven't made their First Communion. But Father, they are such good kids. They work hard, they are kind to everyone, they are involved in community services. In some cases the whole family has gone over to a fundamentalist church and they are very active there. Where did we go wrong? How did we fail them?

The questions are heart-wrenching. I usually begin by assuring the parents and grandparents that they most probably did not fail or "go wrong." They gave them the best they could. But nowadays there are so many other influences, job demands, and cultural pressures to relegate religion to a low priority or ignore it altogether. Many of these young adults are still religious or spiritual in their own way. They may even pray and read the Bible. But they have little regard for what they call "organized religion." Being part of a church community just isn't important to them. It is all part of the American spirit of individualism. It is an enormous challenge for the institutional church to convince these independent-minded people of the importance of being part of a spiritual community, that being a follower of Christ necessarily includes becoming connected to the church he founded—what the scriptures call not "an institution" but "the Body of Christ" (Rom 12:5; 1 Cor 12:27; Eph 1:23).

But that could be the subject of a whole other book. Meanwhile, what can parents do for their non-practicing children? I always begin by telling them, first of all, don't nag. Constant criticism, scoldings, or warnings about their not attending church will only serve to deepen their resistance. (I usually see heads nodding in agreement at this point.) But then I go on to say: "Don't stop loving them; and don't stop praying for them." I remind them that love is the most convincing "proof" of the validity of their own faith. In their honest, quiet moments these adult children may come to the realization: Mom and Dad have something that gives them a peaceful and loving spirit; that's something I want for myself. I also remind the parents that God loves their children even more than they do. So they need to keep praying, keep commending them to the care of God.

But then I usually add: There's one more thing you might do. Once in a while, "throw them a zinger." That is, ask them a question that might make them think. For example: "You're doing so many good things for yourselves and your children—we're proud of you for that. But what are you doing to nourish your (and their) spiritual life? How are you tending your souls?" Or, "You know, the Third Commandment says, 'Remember to keep holy the Lord's day.' What are you doing to keep the Lord's day (Sunday) holy? From what you're telling us, it sounds like it's just another day." Or, "The other day little Billy and Stacy asked us, 'How come Mom and Dad don't take us to church on Sundays like our friends do?' What do you tell them when they ask *you* that?" Of course, you have to be careful when and how you throw those zingers. It has to be done in a gentle, loving way, not in a harsh or critical tone of voice. And, if the adult children have joined another church, it will do no good to berate or put down that church. If they begin to attack the Catholic Church, it would help you to be equipped to answer their objections reasonably. We will discuss this further in the final chapter of this book.

Let me add a word here about ministry to young adults. This is a concern not only of parents but of the entire church. One of the best known people working in this area is Fr. John Cusick, director of Young Adult Ministry for the Archdiocese of Chicago. He is also a member of the pastoral team at Old St. Patrick's Church near downtown Chicago, a community that regularly draws large numbers of young adults. A few years ago Fr. Cusick was interviewed by Dick Westley in a publication called *In The Meantime*. Some of the points he made are so interesting that I would like to share them.

First of all, Fr. Cusick believes that the primary "target group" for evangelization today is not the alienated, nor the disenfranchised, nor even the ex-Catholics. No, he says, the primary group should be our own young people. They haven't had a chance to be alienated. They haven't even had a chance to be disenfranchised, because they are waiting to be asked to be franchised. Which is why (and this is a second point), when he began to do young adult ministry, he did not offer events or programs and invite young people to come. Instead, he went out and gathered groups of them together and said, "Talk to me about who you are and about the Catholic Church." (You see, evangelization begins with listening). He would take notes while these bright young adults would talk about "an incredible hunger for some sense of meaning in their lives." Or, as they put it, "Does it make any difference that I'm around?" They are looking for meaning and purpose rather than for dogmas and rules. They don't much care for institutions, but if the church will offer them an atmosphere of acceptance and an opportunity to explore spiritual issues, they will connect. Cusick doesn't think they are hostile to religion or even irreligious. They are definitely open to spirituality. What we need to do is ask the right questions and facilitate their search. Eventually they may discover the importance of a meaningful system of beliefs (dogmas) and a set of guidelines (rules) for good moral living.

He also believes there are at least two groups of young adults: the twenty-somethings and the thirty-somethings, each with quite different agendas. The twenty-somethings are concerned about forming relationships and finding their place in the world of work. The first issue raises questions about the meaning of sexuality, the difference between self-gratification and genuine love, and the pain of rejection. The workplace also confronts young adults with ethical and moral questions. Furthermore, when they come to realize that their career is not their God, they have to begin to face the question, "Who am I apart from my roles?" Seen in their proper perspective, these are all religious questions. The other group, the thirty-somethings, have pretty well bought into the American dream of success and upward mobility. But then the question arises, "Does economic or vocational success equal happiness?" In their honest moments, many will answer in the negative. Then the search for deeper meaning can begin. But there is another question. This is the group that has postponed marriage and children; now, with children arriving comes the question of what values they should transmit to them.

What does the church have to offer them? Speaking for myself I would answer: a great deal. We have a centuries-old body of teaching about marriage and family, about human sexuality, about the dignity of the human person, about the meaning of sickness and death in human experience. But Fr. Cusick would say: we must not waste energy scolding young adults for not being in church or joining the parish. Rather, we invite them to talk, to dialogue, to share their concerns in an atmosphere of respect and welcome. Then we invite them to reflect on the wisdom found in the scriptures and the church's rich tradition. For many young adults, these could well become "moments of return"—to faith, to spirituality, perhaps even to sacramental life within the church community. Fr. Cusick and Katherine DeVries have just published an excellent book titled *The Basic Guide to Young Adult Ministry* (Orbis Books, 2001).

Lest we lose perspective, let me repeat what I said earlier: Evangelization does not mean proselytizing. We Catholics will not go around trying to draw committed, practicing Protestants, Jews, Muslims, Buddhists or others away from their communities. If we have opportunities, we can certainly share with them the riches we have found in our Catholic Christianity and invite them to take a look themselves. Even more so if we find they are non-practicing or are dissatisfied with their own religion. But we are not going to pressure or harass anyone. We have more than enough to do by way of outreach to inactive Catholics and those who have no faith community.

What we have been looking at in this chapter is the second goal for evangelization proposed by the U.S. bishops in their 1992 Pastoral Plan, *Go and Make Disciples*: to invite all people to hear the message of salvation in Jesus Christ and to consider finding a spiritual home in the Catholic community of faith. Surely the Holy Spirit is stirring up, in our time, a variety of initiatives and methods to implement this goal. Above all, we must assure that whatever means we employ, we will always act with love and respect for those we are trying to reach, and with humble awareness that our church is always in need of purification and growth in fidelity to Christ our Savior.

Let me end with an anecdote that I once heard Archbishop Rembert Weakland tell. He was visiting a parish in England, and the pastor related an incident that had just happened that week. A couple had come to the rectory asking how they could become "lapsed Catholics." Puzzled by the request, the pastor asked them to explain. They told him they had recently moved into town. One day a woman came to their door with a plate of cookies to welcome them into the neighborhood. She helped them arrange some furnishings, told them where to find medical and dental services, and shared other bits of useful information. The couple, touched by her warmth and helpful spirit, asked what church she belonged to. "Oh," she said, "I'm a lapsed Catholic." The couple added, "We decided to join her church. Are you the pastor?"

Another sad/funny story, I thought. But I couldn't help thinking, "Wouldn't it be wonderful if every one of our active Catholics could show that kind of welcoming hospitality to the stranger, and willingness to extend themselves in service even without being asked?" That would be evangelization in action.

Evangelizing
the
Culture

In his prophetic document *On Evangelization in the Modern World*, Pope Paul VI called the church to bring the message of the gospel not only to individuals and families but to the whole society:

> The split between the Gospel and culture is without a doubt the drama of our time, just as it was of other times. Therefore every effort must be made to ensure a full evangelization of culture, or more correctly of cultures. They have to be regenerated by an encounter with the Gospel (n. 20).

Another way of saying it might be: It is very difficult for individuals and families to live according to the gospel of Jesus if the surrounding culture is proclaiming and living by some other gospel or ideology. Later in the document the pope insists that proclamation of the gospel must be accompanied by efforts to promote a more just and human social order:

> . . . How in fact can one proclaim the new commandment [of love] without promoting in justice and in peace the true, authentic advancement of man? We ourselves have taken care to point this out [in a previous document] by recalling that it is impossible to accept that in evangelization one

could or should ignore the importance of the problems so much discussed today concerning justice, liberation, development and peace in the world. This would be to forget the lesson which comes to us from the Gospel concerning love of our neighbor who is suffering and in need (n. 31).

The above insight is sometimes expressed in the simplistic slogan: "You can't preach the gospel to people with empty stomachs; first you have to feed them." We may also have to help them obtain clean drinking water, better sanitation, more adequate health care, better education, decent housing and working conditions. We may have to help them stand up for their human rights against oppressive governments. At the same time, Pope Paul VI did not want to reduce evangelization to a merely secular endeavor. He insisted that the transcendent, spiritual dimension of the gospel not be muted. "If this were so," he wrote, "the Church would lose her fundamental meaning. Her message of liberation would no longer have any originality and would easily be open to . . . manipulation by ideological systems and political parties. She would have no more authority to proclaim freedom as in the name of God" (n. 32). Therefore, evangelization must always include the call to turn away from sin and evil, to open minds and hearts to the message of salvation in Jesus Christ, invitation to enter the communion of the church, and the promise of eternal life.

When our American bishops issued their pastoral plan for evangelization in the United States, they also insisted on the societal dimension of the gospel. "The Gospel," they said, "also speaks to society itself, with its values, goals, and systems. The Gospel must overflow from each heart until the presence of God transforms all human existence. Sometimes this means that, as believers, we must confront the world as did the prophets of old, pointing out the claims of God to societies that are blind to God" (*Go and Make Disciples*, p. 3).

RECLAIM THE FIRE

So the bishops state as Goal III of their pastoral plan: "To foster Gospel values in our society, promoting the dignity of the human person, the importance of the family, and the common good of our society, so that our nation may continue to be transformed by the saving power of Jesus Christ." The bishops are aware of a serious problem for evangelization. It is difficult for contemporary Americans to hear the gospel of Christ because there are so many other "gospels" competing for their attention and loyalty. It is difficult to live spiritually when so much in the culture is unspiritual; to live simply when the culture rewards luxury; to be gentle when toughness and violence are the norm; to be chaste when your peers are urging you to indulge your sexuality; to be forgiving when so many others are bent on getting even; to have compassion for the poor when it seems more politically correct to be mean-spirited.

But the bishops are careful not to condemn U.S. culture wholesale. They note, on the one hand, that there is much that can be affirmed in our culture: the nation's instinctual religiousness, its prizing of freedom and religious liberty, its openness to immigrants, its inspiring idealism. On the other hand, they point out, "our country can be faulted for its materialism, sexism, racism, consumerism, its individualism run wild, its disregard of human life, its endless chase after empty fads and immediate pleasures" (p. 9).

Goal III follows upon the first two: the appreciation of our faith and our sharing it with others ought to lead to the transformation of our society. This is a unique feature of Catholic evangelization. Where other faith traditions are content to focus on conversion of the individual and ignore the wider social context, Catholics believe that true evangelization is not complete or even possible apart from a powerful witness of justice, peace, and promotion of the common good.

Forms of Societal Evangelization

What are some forms that evangelization of society might take? Let us start with one that Catholics will readily recognize: *efforts to uphold the value of human life.* Pope John Paul II has often spoken eloquently about "the Gospel of Life" as opposed to "the Culture of Death" so prevalent in industrialized societies today. Beginning with life in the womb, we are called to protect the most vulnerable members of our species. We firmly and unequivocally reject abortion as a solution to any kind of so-called "problem pregnancy." We believe that abortion is a direct attack on an innocent human life. At the same time, we pledge ourselves to help girls and women whose pregnancy may create hardship—financial, medical, or emotional. I am often filled with admiration when I read about a diocese that pledges financial help so that mothers may have adequate health care for themselves and their newborns. Or when I hear of agencies and clinics that offer counseling and other services for those who are pregnant out of wedlock. I am proud of organizations like Project Rachel that provide opportunities for reconciliation and healing for women who have had an abortion. I applaud the pro-life organizations that make use of persuasion and solid moral reasoning to help people understand and reject the evil of abortion. These are not only pro-life activities; they are also forms of evangelization.

Another way we try to uphold the value of human life is by resistance to capital punishment. More and more we are seeing that "an eye for an eye" or a life for a life is not consistent with the Gospel of Life. With modern methods of DNA testing, an increasing number of inmates on death row have been found innocent of the crime for which they were supposed to undergo death. That fact alone should make us hesitant to decree the death of a prisoner, if not lead us to reject it altogether. But even more, the death penalty is a denial of our belief in the sacredness of human life, including the life of a criminal. "Two wrongs don't make a right" is a proverb even young children will invoke. Granted that the victim's life was unjustly taken away, what do we gain by killing the killer? If he or she is allowed to live, there is at least a chance for spiritual conversion. It is this kind of moral reasoning that has led our American bishops, in their recent convocation, to reject the death penalty as an appropriate form of justice. Again, the church is trying to proclaim a consistent ethic of life across the board.

That consistency also extends to the end of life. We Catholics believe that life is a gift of God; it is not to be terminated by the will of human beings. Therefore, all forms of "assisted suicide" are wrong. There is no requirement to prolong life with extraordinary and costly measures; but that is not the same as deliberately ending a life deemed to be "burdensome." As pressure mounts to allow individuals or physicians to terminate life, the church continues to resist. Happily, this had hastened the discovery of various methods of pain management, palliative care, hospice care, and other forms of enabling people to die with dignity. All these efforts to uphold the sacredness of human life are forms of evangelizing the culture.

Another way evangelization takes place is by *upholding ethical and moral values* in the world of business, labor, and the professions. Here is where the Catholic Church has a long record of social teaching, going back at least as far as Pope Leo XIII. The basic premise might be expressed this way: every form of human endeavor has some ethical-moral dimension. It is not right for either business or labor to pursue their own interests with no regard for the rights of each other or of the wider public. Similarly, while science has the noble goal of discovering the secrets of nature and using its knowledge for the improvement of human life, it must not do so at the expense of human dignity.

The horrors of the Nazi and Communist regimes have shown us what can happen when scientists are encouraged to conduct life-threatening experiments on human persons. In our own time, church leaders have often spoken out against the arms race among nations and against the immorality of using science and technology to develop ever more sophisticated weapons of mass destruction. These prophetic and sometimes unpopular teachings are another form of evangelization.

But sometimes the most powerful evangelizing actions are those of individuals and small groups acting out of their moral convictions. Here are several examples:

ᴗ I personally know a man who turned down an offer to work a second-shift (evening) job at a considerably higher pay scale because, as he said, "it's more important for me to be at home evenings with my wife and children."

ᴗ I know the owner of a three-shift packaging plant who shuts it down (at significant loss) every Sunday so that his workers will be free to attend church and be with their families on Sundays.

ᴗ There are "whistle blowers" who report ethical misconduct in their workplace, often at the risk of harassment or even job loss.

ᴗ There are scientists who have left lucrative jobs in the laboratory when they were asked to conduct research or experiments that could be harmful to persons or to the environment.

ᴗ There are human rights advocates such as Amnesty International that serve as the conscience for government criminal justice systems around the world.

ᴗ There are groups of advocates for homeless people, for immigrants, and for those who are trapped in poverty. These groups keep the faces of disadvantaged people continually before us and our government leaders so that we will not forget them. At the same time, they lobby for policies that will be more just and humane for those who are needy.

〰 Many individuals and groups today are concerned about protecting the natural environment against the tendency of peoples and nations to exploit natural resources without regard for long-term consequences.

Many of these groups are church-based or at least are imbued with a Christian worldview. But even if they are not, we applaud their efforts because they are truly working to bring about a better social order. And this, we believe, reflects the plan of God for creation and for the people of the world. In my talks to parish groups I often state Goal III of the bishops' pastoral plan for evangelization in these words: "To work together with all people of good will to help transform society with the values of the gospel." We are truly evangelizing when we join hands and voices with those who are trying to create a more just and peaceful society. As Jesus once said, "Whoever is not against you is for you" (Lk 9:50).

Workplace Evangelization

Still another form of societal evangelization is the growing emphasis today on *spirituality in the workplace*. In some ways this has been a reaction against the tendency to separate the world of work from the rest of life, including one's spiritual-moral life. We are beginning to see how unnecessary and even harmful such a split can be. After all, people nowadays may spend up to half their waking hours at work. There ought to be some way to connect all that energy with one's deeper goals and life values. There has to be more to work than satisfying employers and bringing home a salary.

"Spirituality in the workplace" is not necessarily studying the Bible or praying together during lunch hour, though some workers have adopted that practice. More broadly, it means doing whatever we can to make the workplace more human and conducive to growth for the workers as well as more responsible to the public. It is embodied first of all in the ways that people are treated. Is there an atmosphere of mutual respect between employees and supervisors, and among employees themselves? Is there zero tolerance for sexual harassment, for gender, racial, and ethnic discrimination? How are grievances handled? Are efforts made to minimize stress in the workplace?

Recently I heard a fine talk by the CEO of a small company. He began by asking, "How do you measure success?" Then he named the usual answers: financial growth, productivity, market share, portfolio gain, technology advances. Without negating any of these, he stated his own bottom-line conviction: "Success is measured most by the way our people are treated." And he quoted the chairman of the Harley-Davidson Company: "Invest in people. They are the only competitive advantage." The speaker went on to talk about the concept of "servant leadership" articulated by Robert K. Greenleaf (*Servant Leadership*, Paulist Press, 1983), describing it as someone who can help you to become the best you can be. He quoted another employer who said, "I think spirituality comes across in our actions and value systems and language." Speaking of language, it can be a powerful indicator of how human the workplace is. I know a woman whose daughter told her there is so much negative talk going on in her workplace that she caught herself slipping into the very same behavior patterns she hates.

Jesuit writer James Martin relates an incident that happened when he was a layman in the corporate world. He had to confront a manager who was planning to fire one of his employees. Ironically, the employee had just received an incentive award for outstanding performance on the job. Martin told the manager it seemed bizarre that they should suddenly fire one of their top employees. "I don't care," the manager said, "I don't like him!" Martin then reminded him that the man had consistently done a good job for twenty years and that not liking someone was not a valid reason for dismissal. None of that seemed to matter. Finally he said, "Have some compassion. The guy's got a family." The manager's reply stunned him: "To hell with compassion!" he shouted. For Martin, that episode aptly symbolized the ethos of the company and ultimately led him to decide to leave the corporate world and enter religious life (Reported in *America*, July 1-8, 2000).

The point for us: evangelization must somehow touch the lives of people where they work. So, when individuals strive for excellence in their work, they are evangelizing. When they treat their co-workers, customers, and suppliers with respect and dignity, they are evangelizing. When they insist on fair treatment for everyone in the workplace, they are evangelizing. When they try to insure that their products and services are safe and free of deception, they are evangelizing. When they insist that work practices are not harmful to the natural environment, they are evangelizing. Why? Because they are bringing ethical and moral values to bear upon an all-important area of human life. In a very real sense, and perhaps without being fully aware of it, they are witnessing to the gospel of Jesus Christ.

Parish-Based Efforts

Since this book is intended primarily for parishes, let me turn now to some parish-based forms of societal evangelization. The first examples that come to mind are those activities that are traditionally called "the works of mercy." Most parishes, I believe, have developed some forms of outreach to the poor and needy people in their midst. The parish will have a food pantry and a room full of used clothing. Some will serve a meal at the parish once a week (sometimes more), or members will help serve it at another location. Some parishes band with other churches to offer shelter to the homeless. Others have a ministry of visitation to prisoners. Still others engage the services of a parish nurse to oversee the needs of elderly and homebound persons in the neighborhood. All of these efforts are evangelizing, in the sense of making visible the compassion of Jesus in today's world and communicating the message that the parish is concerned about more than its own members.

Some parishes encourage the formation of support groups for persons with other kinds of needs: separated and divorced; widowed; those who have suffered the loss of a loved one; caregivers; recovering alcoholics; people living with AIDS or with cancer. Other groups are formed to support families with young children. Nowadays there are so many negative forces from the culture that families need all the help and wisdom they can get to stay focused on Christian values. What are parents to do, for example, when children want to dress in the provocative styles of pop stars or listen to music or attend movies that are sexually explicit, violent, and demeaning to women? Often parents can learn from one another by participating in group discussions with peers who share a common gospel vision. Here is an example where people evangelize one another. Indirectly, they are also challenging the culture: "We will not buy into the false and materialistic values that you are propagating." Conversely, these groups also agree to buy from and patronize those businesses that refrain from selling such items and offer positive alternatives. I have nothing but admiration for families who are willing to stand against the show of glitter, smut, and violence paraded around every day by the prevailing culture.

Some parishes, through their Human Service Committee, also have a core of activist members who work to bring about changes in some of the unjust systems and structures of society. So, for example, besides providing shelter for the homeless, these groups will try to determine why there are so many homeless people or why there are not enough public shelters to care for them. They will then take constructive action: informing the public, holding demonstrations, talking with city/county officials, writing letters, lobbying state legislatures. Similarly, if more people are being denied health care, the group will try to find out why and take whatever action seems appropriate to correct the situation. Although at first blush these actions may not seem like evangelization, in a very real sense they are. These Christians are bringing the light of the gospel to bear upon situations or systems that are dehumanizing. Pope Paul VI encouraged just such forms of activity when he wrote:

> [The church] is trying more and more to encourage large numbers of Christians to devote themselves to the liberation of all. She is providing these Christian "liberators" with the inspiration of faith, the motivation of fraternal love, a social teaching which true Christians cannot ignore and which they must make the foundation of their wisdom . . . in order to translate it concretely into forms of action, participation, and commitment (*On Evangelization in the Modern World*, n. 38).

Evangelizing in the Central City

Sometimes I am asked, "OK, but how do you do evangelization in the central city?" Underlying the question there is, at times, an unspoken assumption: Most churches in the central city are located in neighborhoods that are largely African-American, and "those people" are all connected to Baptist or Pentecostal churches. For one thing, central city neighborhoods often house predominantly Latino populations and sometimes Asian-American or other ethnic groups. For another, it is simply not true that all African-Americans belong to small Protestant churches. The fact is, a large number of urban blacks are unchurched (I have heard figures as high as fifty percent and higher). In any case, the mission to evangelize is as urgent in the central city as anywhere else—if not more so. I am certainly no authority on central city parish ministry. But I have had numerous conversations with fellow Capuchin friars who have spent the bulk of their ministry in central city parishes. I will focus on predominantly African-American parishes here in the context of evangelizing the culture.

The first thing I have learned from my conversations is this: Historically, the lives of African-Americans have been closely bound to their churches. It was often church ministers who took leadership roles in the community, including the struggle for equal rights. Church worship, prayer and Bible reading, the singing of hymns—all gave voice to the sufferings and the hopes of the people. The churches have always been natural gathering places for African-Americans. Unfortunately, the Catholic Church has lagged far behind in ending segregation and in promoting the civil rights of black people. Therefore, one of the primary forms of Catholic evangelization in the central city must be a clear and unequivocal commitment to racial equality and an end to all forms of discrimination. Perhaps one advantage Catholic churches in the central city may have is the fact that they nearly always have a number of parishioners who are from the Latino and Anglo communities, providing an opportunity to experience and model a multicultural community of faith. Of course, the same reality may be a challenge for the various groups to work together.

Another insight I gained from living in the central city and talking with church ministers is the importance of good liturgy. "Good" here means, among other things, worship that arises out of the people's cultural heritage and gives expression to it. This includes African-American music and dance forms, preaching that is high-spirited and interactive, and an atmosphere that is more relaxed and informal. There is a strong emphasis on welcome and hospitality. It is important to connect with one another, to learn names, to socialize for a while before and after the Mass. Such liturgy evangelizes those who participate. They feel at home in the house of God. They feel part of the church family. They hear how the great stories and themes of scripture relate to their own lives. They get the message that they are to bring something of what they have experienced into their homes and workplaces. It is the kind of worship to which they will invite their unchurched friends and neighbors.

There is one more aspect of evangelization in the central city that I would like to highlight: the importance of the parish being closely connected with the life of the neighborhood. Let me illustrate this by means of two "case studies":

Grace Lutheran Church is a central city church in San Francisco. When a new pastor arrived the church was dying—only a few active members and a $23,000 deficit. The surrounding community, living in fear of crime, perceived the church as irrelevant at best and oppressive at worst. Four years later, membership doubled and the budget was balanced. Most of the new members came from the ranks of the previously unchurched. Members who once felt demoralized now recount overhearing perfect strangers talk about the great things Grace Lutheran is doing in the community.

What turned it around? As the pastor describes it, it wasn't any high-powered, sophisticated marketing program. It was "two big ears and a caring heart." Or better, a number of such combinations. What he did was train a small group of active members to visit the neighborhood with an open attitude and a simple approach: "We're from Grace Lutheran Church and we're concerned about the people in this neighborhood. Could you tell us: What are *your* needs or concerns?" Maybe not those exact words, but that was the general idea.

The purpose of the visit was not to recruit new members, but to do a needs assessment. It turned out that the needs and the self-interests of the neighborhood were three-fold: stopping the illegal sale of cars on Sunset Blvd.; stopping white supremacist activity at a nearby park; and the need for more police. This needs assessment was valuable in itself, for it gave a positive message to the community about the church. "As we went door-to-door to listen to our neighbors," the pastor says, "we heard a common theme: 'This is the first time someone took the time to learn what I wanted or needed or how I felt.'" Two big ears and a caring heart.

But listening was not enough. Follow-up action was a necessary second step. So the church offered a couple of town hall meetings where neighbors could come and express their concerns in a public forum and explore some strategies for having their needs met. The next step was to get the alderman and City Hall to attend one of these meetings (members of the Common Council and even the mayor came). All it took to get their attention was to count the potential votes (*their* self-interest) and see the discipline and focus of the community. Within three years the problems were solved:

🕊 More police were added to the district as well as a new captain who was more community-minded and sensitive than the previous one;

🔥 The police routed the supremacist gang from the park;

🔥 They enforced a state law prohibiting the sale of cars on the streets. As a result, crime went down. Thieves could no longer pretend to be purchasing cars while they were really casing out homes or watching for purses to snatch. A prostitution ring also disappeared once the cars were gone.

This effort at community organizing produced several important payoffs. First, it gave the people a sense of their own power to affect and change their lives for the better; they could actually create systemic change, not just Band-Aid solutions. Second, it connected Grace Lutheran Church to the neighborhood and made it a vital force for good in the community. And third, it created bonds and relationships among people, many of whom wanted to work toward long range goals to prevent problems from arising in the future, and who wanted to become part of something larger than themselves. And these were the people who eventually joined or rejoined the church.

When I read about this I said to myself, "Now there is an evangelizing church. It is reaching out and bringing the good news of God's presence into a troubled neighborhood." It is "working with people of good will to transform society with the values of the Gospel." It sounds very much like Goal III of the U.S. Bishops' *Go and Make Disciples*. Here is another case study:

Reformation Lutheran Church is located in Milwaukee's inner city and is led by a dynamic Anglo pastor, the Rev. Mick Roschke. I was privileged to hear him speak and I read his book *A Church of the People: Strategies of Urban Ministry* (privately published, 1997). He is convinced that the local church must address specific problems faced by the community, based on a Christian faith expressed in love. So the church needs to be closely connected to life in the neighborhood.

Among other strategies, Reformation Lutheran makes use of "neighborhood ministers." These are people who reside in the neighborhood and are gifted with the ability to listen and care for people. Often they are able to touch people who feel alienated from the church or are ashamed to come into the church. These lay ministers are paid a modest salary based on thirty-five hours a week. The pastor refers certain people to the neighborhood minister who then visits and tries to connect them with the Christian community. Sometimes the ministers develop their own contacts and follow through. The problems they address are multiple: budgeting money, child neglect, troubled children, alcohol and drug addiction, and lack of awareness of community resources. Neighborhood ministers are an integral part of the parish staff and receive support from the pastor and the rest of the staff.

Another strategy Pastor Roschke uses is to make connections with other neighborhood institutions. For example, he meets with the principal of the local public school to discuss ways the church and school can work together. He spends time in the school library, the cafeteria, the teachers' lounge—getting to know students and teachers. And, since children often spend hours in the local public library, the pastor makes it a point to visit there also. He contacts local business places, including banks. The church, he believes, should do its banking locally. He meets with bank personnel to find out how much money is being reinvested in the neighborhood, especially as it relates to housing rehabilitation and loans to the poor.

Through these efforts the church becomes highly visible in the neighborhood. Moreover, it can take prophetic stands against various forms of evil. Reformation Lutheran occasionally holds town hall meetings where neighbors can share concerns about what is going on around them. In one instance, church members decided to gather after the Good Friday service to pray in front of a drug house that was operating in the neighborhood. The attention this generated, along with calls and letters to the media and city officials, resulted in the closing of the drug house and its remodeling by the city into needed, affordable housing.

In all this, the church is careful not to lose its spiritual purpose. Sunday worship is carefully planned and celebrated. Every Wednesday is designated as "Education Night" for all ages, including adults. The classes are divided according to age for the children, while adults have an opportunity to study and discuss some topic pertaining to Christian faith. Each Thursday night is set aside for "Community Bible Study," which is open to everyone, including non-members of the parish. Twice a month there is also a meeting of "House Churches"—small groups where people share faith, pray for and support each other in their spiritual journeys. Each Friday night a community meal ("Bread of Life") is served in the church hall. Members mingle freely with guests. And every Saturday morning there is a Men's Breakfast and Bible Study.

It is no wonder that Reformation Lutheran is one of the growing congregations in the central city. But it would not be difficult to name others. In Milwaukee we find St. Anthony and the tri-parish cluster of St. Michael-St. Rose-St. Francis of Assisi having a multi-cultural blend of Latinos, Anglos, Asians, and African-Americans. Likewise in Chicago, St. Sabina's and Holy Angels, and in Detroit, Sacred Heart and St. Charles Borromeo are growing congregations in the central city. These and many others are vibrant, evangelizing parishes in neighborhoods that are often abandoned by the rest of the community. They are centers of spirituality and worship as well as centers of outreach to the poor and marginalized people within their borders. They have caught the fire, and we salute them.

Becoming
an
Evangelizing
Parish

By this time readers may be asking, "Okay, but how can all this become part of prish life and activity? What would *an evangelizing parish* look like?" Some years ago, in response to that question, I put together what I called "A Vision for an Evangelizing Parish." It turned out to have seven points. Now, having read Stephen Covey's *Seven Habits of Highly Effective People,* we might dub these "Seven Habits of Evangelizing Parishes."

1. *An evangelizing parish is a community that is convinced it has a precious gift to share: the Gospel of Jesus Christ.* The parish does not exist for itself; it is purpose-driven and mission-driven. Howard Clinebell begins his book on pastoral counseling with a parable originally put forward by Theodore Wedel. It describes a dangerous seacoast where shipwrecks were common. A small group of people built a little life-saving station with one boat for rescue operations. Because of the great dedication of the group, the station became well known and admired for saving many lives. In time it attracted more members, some of whom were dissatisfied with the crude building and equipment. They raised money and replaced it with a fine building and

furniture, which soon became a favorite gathering place for the members. Since fewer members were now interested in going out on life-saving missions, they hired lifeboat crews to do the work. At the next meeting there was a split in the membership. Most wanted to stop the life-saving activities as being a hindrance to the normal social life of the group. A few others insisted that the place was still called a life-saving station, so that was their primary purpose. They were told that if they wanted to continue doing that, they could set up their own life-saving station down the coast. So they did. With the passage of time, the same phenomenon occurred. The station evolved into a club, and another life-saving operation was started. And if you visit that coast today, it is said, you will find a number of exclusive clubs along the shore. Shipwrecks are still frequent in those waters, but most of the people drown. (Quoted in Howard Clinebell, *Basic Types of Pastoral Care and Counseling*, Abingdon, 1984, p. 14).

The perennial temptation of the parish (as well as of the church itself) is to become a comfortable club rather than a center of grace, healing, and salvation. If Jesus Christ and his gospel are not at the center of the parish's life, it will quickly become irrelevant. After all, people can find fulfillment of their physical and emotional needs in any number of places: the health club, the shopping mall, the psychotherapist's office, the investment firm. But where will they find a sense of meaning and purpose for their lives? Where will they find something—or Someone—to believe in? Something to hope for, to help make sense of their suffering and the inevitability of death? That is what Jesus and his gospel have to offer. And that must always be the primary focus of the parish. As Pope Paul VI stated so powerfully:

. . . The presentation of the Gospel message is not an optional contribution for the Church. It is the duty incumbent on her by the command of the Lord Jesus, so that people can believe and be saved. This message is indeed necessary. It is unique. It cannot be replaced. . . . It is a question of people's salvation. It is the beauty of the revelation that it represents. It brings with it a wisdom that is not of this world. It is able by itself to stir up faith—faith that rests on the power of God. . . . (*On Evangelization in the Modern World*, n. 5)

It is not difficult to feel the passion in the pope's words.

2. *An evangelizing parish is one that listens to God's word in the Scriptures and allows itself to be encouraged and challenged by that word.* Sometimes fundamentalist and evangelical Christians claim to be "Bible-believing" churches, with the implication that we Catholics are not; instead, we put our faith in our traditions, rituals, and rules. Whatever truth there might have been in that stereotype at one time, it is surely fading fast. We Catholics are drawing our faith and our spirituality more and more from the word of God in scripture. This is evidenced in the three-year cycle of biblical readings for Sunday Eucharist, as well as in the numerous Bible study groups meeting in our parishes and in the daily Scripture meditation booklets currently on the market.

Note that the evangelizing parish allows itself to be both "encouraged" and "challenged" by the word of God. This implies that preachers and music ministers know how to lift up the biblical words and stories so they will comfort those who are hurting and affirm the parish for what it is already doing well. At the same time, they are willing to challenge those who may be growing complacent and self-satisfied, and to call the parish to the next level of outreach or expansion.

Parishioners are always moved when they can see themselves and their parish reflected in the biblical passages that are being proclaimed.

3. *An evangelizing parish is one that celebrates God's action in the lives of people through the eucharist and the other sacraments.* This characteristic is closely linked to the previous one. The difference is: it highlights not only the word of God but also the actions of God. And not only God's actions in history, but also in the present. The eucharist and all the sacraments are primarily sacred actions. They recall God's great deeds in human history, but they signify the continued divine activity in our present lives. As St. Augustine said in one of his homilies on the sacraments: It is Christ who baptizes at the font; it is Christ who forgives sins in reconciliation; in the eucharist it is Christ who offers himself in perfect love and sacrifice to the Father, and gives himself totally to us in communion; it is Christ who heals the sick, it is Christ who blesses the human love of husband and wife. This is why Vatican II insisted that all the sacraments must include the reading of scripture in their celebrations, so that they may be seen as the actions of Christ continuing in space and time. Again, when the prayers, the gestures, the words, and the music can connect the scriptures with the human situation of the people, the sacraments can be powerful evangelizing moments.

4. *An evangelizing parish is a community that reaches out to hurting people of all kinds, in order to bring God's love into their lives.* One Protestant pastor put it very well when he said, "If the church does not meet the needs of the people, it will not grow. We aim to have a comprehensive ministry. We say, 'See a need and meet it; find a hurt and heal it.' Howard Clinebell recalls how he looked out over his congregation one Sunday and became aware of the many troubled people gathered there: a man who had admitted his wife to a mental

hospital the week before; a young wife deeply depressed by the tragic death of her husband; a couple whose child was recently diagnosed with leukemia; an alcoholic struggling with his addiction; a couple whose marriage appeared to be breaking apart; a high school boy whose girlfriend was pregnant; a man facing surgery for a condition he suspected was malignant; a woman struggling to recover from a painful divorce (*Basic Types of Pastoral Care and Counseling*, 1984). And these were only the ones he knew about. How many others were carrying burdens unknown to him? And, I would add, how many others are similarly troubled but are not present in church?

We are reminded of how the heart of Jesus was "moved with compassion" at the sight of the crowd around him, because they were "troubled and abandoned" like sheep without a shepherd (Mt 9:36). But no pastor can single-handedly reach out to all the hurting people in the parish, which is why many parishes have developed ministries of care under the direction of deacons, women religious, and lay ministers. Whether they are called Stephen Ministries, Befrienders, Compassionate Friends, Parish Nurses— the mission is the same: to identify parishioners in need and minister to them in the name of Christ and the parish community. When a parish does this, even on a small scale, it is truly evangelizing.

Another dream I've had for some time is that the parish might become known as a center where troubled people can gather for prayer as well as support. I envision lay-led prayer services for various groups that share common problems: those who are grieving the loss of a loved one; those living with cancer or other chronic illness; caregivers of handicapped children or elderly parents; those recovering from divorce; survivors of sexual and/or domestic abuse. The list could go on. These would be prayer services, not therapy or support groups as such. The format could be very simple: an opening prayer; a reading from scripture; invitation to participants to share their reflections on the scripture and/or some of their personal story; time to pray silently or aloud for healing; recitation of a psalm or some other prayer in common. The point is that people need to know that they are not alone in their pain and suffering, but are linked with others who are bearing similar burdens. They need to know that the compassion and healing power of Jesus are available to them, just as they were to the people of gospel times. And they are pleased to find this in their local church community.

5. *An evangelizing parish is involved in working for justice, for the rights and dignity of all peoples, including the poor and marginalized of society.* We have already discussed this aspect of evangelization in the previous chapter. Here we simply want to highlight again the absolute necessity for the local parish church to be continually aware of its wider mission. Even if a parish is located in a suburban or affluent neighborhood, it is called to be mindful of the poor and disadvantaged people of the world. Many parishes have "adopted" or "twinned" with a needy parish, domestic or foreign, assisting it with monetary donations and/or needed skills. Ideally, the relationship is reciprocal: the needy parish enriches the other parish by sharing its people's spiritual and cultural gifts. Other middle class and affluent parishes make it a point to educate their people about the systemic causes of injustice and use their resources to help bring about change. As one person put it, "Our pastor feeds us—then we go out into the world."

6. *An evangelizing parish is one that makes known the Good News of Jesus to others and invites them into the Catholic faith community.* Again, we have discussed this at some length in the chapter on reaching out to inactive Catholics and unchurched people. I recently

came across an article written by Archbishop Michael J. Sheehan of Santa Fe entitled "Quenching Spiritual Thirst: The Need to Reach Out to the Parched" (*Be* magazine, July-August 2000). He told how he was at the cathedral for the Easter Vigil and was talking before Mass with the people who were about to be baptized and received into the church that night. Among them was a young couple. The man said he had been an atheist before. The archbishop asked him why he decided to become a Catholic. The young man said he had felt empty. He was thirsty for meaning and values. He began to read C.S. Lewis and became convinced there was a God and that Jesus was indeed his Son who came into the world to save us. Once he was convinced of the truth of Christianity, he felt he should enter the Catholic Church. His young wife, who was holding their two-month-old baby, said her story was about the same. A year later, the archbishop said, this couple was very active in the parish. They are sponsors for another young couple in the RCIA. They are involved in local pro-life efforts. They state openly that their Catholic faith is their greatest treasure. The archbishop's conclusion was that we do a pretty good job of ministering to those already participating in the church. "But how much time do we spend on those not darkening our doorways? The new evangelization . . . calls us to be creative in reaching them as well."

How true. And how many other people are "out there"—with the same spiritual thirst, the same desire to find something solid to anchor them in a fast-paced world, and some community to support them in their spiritual journey? That young couple was strongly self-motivated. But so many others will not take those first steps to find God or to reconnect with the Catholic community all on their own. They will need to meet someone whose own faith is credible and who will take the initiative to ask the spiritual questions: What helps you make sense of life? What do you believe about

God/Jesus? Do you ever pray? How did you happen to drift away from the church and the sacraments? Do you ever miss them? Do you ever think of coming back? What would you need? But, as I've said earlier, it is not just individuals who are called to do this kind of outreach—it is the entire parish community. Which leads to my final point:

7. *An evangelizing parish is a welcoming community that opens itself to receive new members and helps them to know they are valued.* In a previous chapter I named the various ways that the parish needs to communicate the message: "You are welcome here!" I also mentioned some ways parishes have found to reach out and invite inactive Catholics and unchurched people to take a closer look at the parish community. But here I want to focus on another side of the picture. I keep hearing that people who move through the RCIA process and are received into the church too often feel a certain letdown afterwards and even drop out of Mass attendance and parish life. How does this happen? I have a hunch: the new members have not formed meaningful bonds with the regular members. In his fine book *How to Attract and Keep Active Church Members* (Westminster/John Knox, 1992), Donald P. Smith presents research showing the differences between "bonding" churches (those that both attract and retain new members) and "high loss" churches (those that attract but do not retain). In bonding churches the new members are not only warmly welcomed, but they also form affective relationships, usually with the pastor, but always with several active church members. This happens not by chance but by design. New members are strongly encouraged (and in some cases required): 1) to become part of a small faith-sharing group; and 2) to become involved in some form of ministry. Another term used is "high expectations." In our Catholic parishes, it seems, low expectations are more the norm. We often speak glowingly about the

importance of "recognizing and calling forth the gifts" of all members of the Body of Christ. But I wonder how seriously we pursue that noble goal. I mentioned earlier how impressed I was when I attended a workshop at Willow Creek Community Church in Illinois. I learned that the church has over one hundred different ministries and that everyone who joins is required to be involved in at least one of them. Perhaps this is unrealistic for most of our parishes. But are we at least aiming high? Certainly, it would not seem too difficult to connect our new members with a ministry suited to their gifts and interests, especially while their enthusiasm is at a peak.

Process: Becoming an Evangelizing Parish

Now that we have described the vision of an evangelizing parish, how do we get there? I believe there are several principal "actors" that need to be involved in the process. First would be the diocese. Hopefully, the bishop is convinced of the necessity for evangelization as "the essential mission of the Church" (Pope Paul VI, *On Evangelization . . .* , n. 14) and has made that conviction clear both in his teaching and manner of acting. One concrete way would be to establish a diocesan Office for Evangelization. If that is not possible or practical, the diocese can provide resources (written materials, training programs, etc.) for use by the parishes. The next group that needs to be involved is the pastor, along with the pastoral staff and council. As I mentioned in an earlier chapter, without the full support of the pastor, parish evangelization is doomed. On the other hand, if the pastor and staff are on board, it is a pleasure to work with them and the parish council. I will usually suggest gathering for a half-day or full day of retreat together. We study the scriptural and church teachings on evangelization, reflect on the reality of the parish, and begin to form a vision of evangelization for the parish. If that is not possible, I will suggest resources for the staff and council to educate themselves about evangelization.

The next "actor" is the whole parish community. It is essential that they be informed and educated, and become enthused about the evangelizing mission of the parish. This can be achieved in a number of ways: Sunday homilies; a series of bulletin inserts or columns on evangelization; prayers for inactive Catholics and the unchurched in the General Intercessions; asking the homebound members of the parish to pray for the evangelizing ministry; inviting the whole parish to an afternoon (Sunday) or evening session on evangelization. It will take some time before parishioners come to realize that evangelization is not just another one-shot or time-limited program but an ongoing process and part of the parish's "normal business."

One other "actor" would be a parish Evangelization Committee. Its task would be to spearhead the evangelizing ministry of the parish, keep it focused and on track. However, a separate committee may not be necessary if the pastoral staff or some other committee is able and willing to direct evangelization. In any case, it is crucial that the committee not be perceived as "the group that does evangelization" for the parish, while everyone else is exempt. No, evangelization must always be the work of the whole parish. What the committee does is devise concrete strategies and programs (perhaps using the three goals outlined in the U.S. Bishops' Pastoral Plan) and propose them to the parish staff and council for approval. Obviously, committee members need to be selected carefully, lest their personal agendas get in the way of the mission. Also, they will need some formation for their task, as well as support from the pastoral staff and council.

I always tell evangelization committees, "When you start to do evangelization, prepare yourselves for failure." Most of us are new at this. Our first attempts may not be successful. The temptation then is to give up, to conclude that "evangelization doesn't work"—at least in this parish. That notion must be resisted. For even if a given strategy fails, something is always learned. The committee then must reflect on whether the strategy should be modified or perhaps abandoned altogether. The only mistake would be to quit. I am reminded of the well-known story of Thomas Edison's assistant. After trying hundreds of different materials for the filament of the light bulb without success, the exasperated assistant exclaimed, "Mr. Edison, we have failed." But Edison replied, "On the contrary, we have succeeded admirably. We now know that none of those materials will work!" If he had stopped at that point, he would never have invented the light bulb.

Evangelization as an Integrating Vision

One of the problems that evangelization can create for parish staffs, councils, and committees: it can be perceived as another "should," another program to be done, "an added burden on already overworked pastoral staffs," as the U.S. Bishops said in their Pastoral Plan (*Go and Make Disciples*, p. 13). So it may be helpful to re-imagine evangelization as an integrating vision and activity, rather than as a separate ministry. Carol Gura has called this a "convergence" model of evangelization ("The Parish Evangelization Committee: What Works?" in *Catholic Evangelization*, Nov./Dec. 1988). In this approach all the baptized are encouraged to discover and engage in a common mission based on individual gifts and personal responsibilities. And all parish ministries converge around the central mission to evangelize, as illustrated in her diagram that follows on the next page.

Model for Parish Evangelization
Committee/Commission

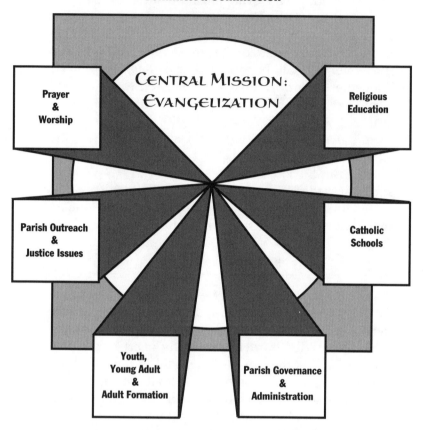

In this model, all parish staff members, parish council and committees keep asking themselves: "How can we be more evangelizing *in what we are already doing?* And how can we keep building on that?" It can be both instructive and gratifying for these groups to see that they are already doing much that is truly evangelizing. They may be aided by asking themselves questions such as the following:

Prayer and Worship: Are our parish liturgies joyfully celebrating the love of God made known to us in the redemptive actions of Jesus Christ? Is our preaching clearly proclaiming these mysteries in ways that touch the real lives of our people? Is our music and style of worship creating an atmosphere of prayerfulness?

Christian Formation: Are we communicating the good news of Jesus Christ to our children and adults in ways that help them to not only understand the truths of our faith but also to commit themselves to being his disciples? Are we encouraging and empowering our parishioners to share their faith with "the ungathered" (inactive Catholics and unchurched people) and invite them to experience our faith community?

Family Life: How are we providing resources for families to foster regular family prayer and religious rituals in the home? Do we sponsor programs for marriage enrichment and parenting skills? How do we provide support for single-parent families, and for separated, divorced, and widowed persons?

Human Concerns: How well are we proclaiming the gospel in action by reaching out to the poor, the marginalized and the hurting members of the parish—and beyond the parish (the works of mercy)? How are we trying to effect change in the social arrangements and systems that keep people poor and marginal (the works of justice)? In a word, are we becoming known as a *caring* parish?

Administrative/Finance Services: How well do our budget allocations reflect our belief that evangelization is "the primary and essential mission" of our parish?

The same kinds of questions can serve as an ongoing reflection tool for every organization in the parish. At the same time, the entire parish is striving to become a warm and welcoming community, one that members would be proud to invite their friends and neighbors to. The word will be out that "some really good things are happening at St. X Parish!"

In this kind of model an evangelization committee may not be necessary, so long as the vision above is being followed. Or, the committee may eventually dissolve itself, because evangelization has become "second nature" at the parish, a lens through which all parish activities are viewed and evaluated. Evangelization has become the dynamism that integrates the diverse gifts and energies of the entire parish.

Becoming a Seeker-Friendly Parish

Earlier in this book I referred to "spiritual seekers"—people who currently are not connected to any church community but are looking for something to help make sense of their lives. Sociologist Wade Clark Roof studied the religious attitudes and behaviors of contemporary baby boomers in *A Generation of Seekers: The Spiritual Journeys of the Baby Boom Generation* (HarperCollins, 1993). Both he and George Gallup in 1988 found that, in spite of the large number of individuals without a church connection, many Americans are seeking a spirituality that gives meaning to their lives and are open to a community that would welcome them.

A few years ago I heard about Willow Creek Community Church in northern Illinois, said to be the fastest-growing Christian church in America. I had an opportunity to attend one of their services on a Saturday evening. The "church" is a huge auditorium that holds 4200 people. That day it was nearly full, as are the three Sunday services. The other thing that struck me was the large number of young people— teens, young adults, parents with young children.

I wanted to learn more about Willow Creek, so I signed up for a Leadership Conference sponsored by the church. Over 3100 people from sixty-two Christian denominations were there for the four-day conference. I learned that the church has made a conscious commitment to reach out to seekers. In fact, the weekend services are all designed to attract people who are presently not active in any church, but are looking for some place where they will be inspired and nourished spiritually. The hope is that gradually they will become fully committed members of Willow Creek. Interestingly, the already committed members are welcome to attend; but they are also expected to come to the Wednesday night service of "worship and teaching." They are also expected to actively invite seekers to attend the weekend service. That is one of their most effective ways of evangelizing, and it accounts for much of the church's growth.

The weekend service is carefully designed to appeal to spiritual seekers, including those who may simply be curious. The curtain rises on a six-piece band playing contemporary music—lively, but not rock. Then the band accompanies a vocalist or two singing a contemporary Christian song. A reader comes out and briefly states the theme for the service: e.g., "Is Life Unfair?" or "Is Family Life Outdated?"—some issue that "grabs" people where they are actually living. Then the reader proclaims a brief passage from scripture around that theme. A small group of actors then comes out and performs a ten- to twelve-minute drama or skit that highlights the theme. This is followed either by a song or a spontaneous prayer. Next someone else comes out and makes the announcements, including the fact that visitors (i.e., seekers) are not expected to contribute to the collection which is taken up at this point. I noted that every effort is made to put no pressure on the seekers or make them uncomfortable. No one tells them to sing along, no one even asks their name (though they are free to take a Visitors Card to fill out and leave in a basket; if they do so, they are contacted within three days). At this point the preacher comes out and gives an interesting sermon based on the Bible and connecting it with the contemporary theme for the day. The service ends with a spontaneous prayer and a closing song. Total time: one hour.

I was impressed by the excellence and "class" with which everything was done. There was a nice blend of seriousness and lightness, of biblical truth and cultural relevance. The service is clearly aimed at unchurched baby boomers and Generation X-ers who are musically and visually oriented. It puts the arts at the service of the gospel. What often happens is that after attending several such services, the seeker feels at home enough to want full membership. Then there is an initiation process: instruction, baptism, placement in a small faith-sharing group, and commitment to one or more of the church's one hundred ministries. As a Catholic, of course, I felt a great sense of letdown at the end because there was no Communion service.

But I found myself wondering: Why couldn't our parishes become more seeker-friendly? Instead of grousing about how the non-denominational megachurches are "stealing" our people, why not try to learn something from them? I often wonder how many seekers are silently present at our weekend liturgies. And whether they walk away with a feeling of "I wouldn't fit here" or "I like what I find here—I'll be back." Could we use our pastoral imagination to appeal to seekers—not only in the Sunday Eucharist but in other programs and services offered by the parish? Could we design a non-eucharistic seeker service, perhaps on Sunday evening, where we would employ the talents of young musicians and actors to situate the preacher's (ordained or non-ordained) biblical message in a contemporary context? Such a service would be open to active parishioners, of course, but it would not be a substitute for the regular Sunday Eucharist. Or, could we utilize some of the dynamics noted above to make our liturgies more attractive to seekers?

Lee Strobel has some interesting and revealing insights into unchurched seekers in his book *Inside the Mind of Unchurched Harry and Mary: How to Reach*

Friends and Family Who Avoid God and the Church (Zondervan, 1993). Strobel was a church dropout and a fast-rising reporter for the *Chicago Tribune* when he rediscovered his need for God and a faith community. The book is an account of his own journey as well as his reflections on the other unchurched people he came to know through his interviews.

Strobel also has some well-aimed challenges for our parishes. For instance, he asks, why is it that Christians are adept at answering the kind of questions posed by other Christians, but inept at responding to the inquiries that seekers want answered? "So Christians end up debating the fine points of whether baptism ought to be by immersion or sprinkling. . . while seekers are voting with their feet and heading away from church" (p. 218). Earlier he had said: "The most effective messages for seekers are those that address their felt needs. Unchurched Harry and Mary want to know if [the Bible] . . . can really give them practical assistance in the trenches of their daily lives. They want to know if it can help them in dealing with their hurts, defusing their anger, resolving their conflicts, easing their fears, overcoming their loneliness . . . understanding themselves, and generally coping with life" (pp. 213-14).

In summary, if the fire of evangelism is ever going to blaze up in our church again, it will have to be kindled at the local parish level. There is an abundance of resources available for pastors and parish lay leaders to help them move closer to the goal of becoming evangelizing parishes. A list of such resources is provided at the end of this book.

Evangelization
and
Apologetics

Many Catholics today are as unfamiliar with the word "apologetics" as they are with evangelization. The word has nothing to do with apologizing. It is simply the science and art of being able to explain our religious beliefs and practices to those who are inquiring. Earlier I noted that the first Christians were encouraged and equipped to do this with their Jewish and Gentile neighbors. Recall the line from the Letter of Peter: "Always be ready to give an explanation to anyone who asks you for a reason for your hope, but do it with gentleness and reverence" (1 Pt 3:15-16). In my earlier chapter on the history of evangelization, I noted that groups like the Paulists and the Catholic Evidence Guild were formed specifically to give clear presentations on Catholic teachings and to defend them against the objections of critics. In the 1940s and '50s some Catholic colleges and even high schools offered courses in apologetics.

Since Vatican II, apologetics has been de-emphasized, probably because it was perceived as defensive and not in accord with the spirit of ecumenism. In recent years, however, there has been a resurgence of interest, fueled largely by the fundamentalist churches' criticisms (and in some cases, attacks) of Catholic teachings. Catholics often find themselves feeling vulnerable and incapable of defending or explaining their beliefs. What do you say, for example, when you are told that the Catholic Church teaches salvation by good works, whereas the Bible says clearly that salvation comes only through faith in Jesus Christ? Or that the Bible alone is our authority in spiritual matters, not the teachings of some merely human authorities like popes and bishops? Or that the Mass and sacraments are superstitious rituals with no power to save us or help us come close to God? Or that our "worship" of Mary and the saints is blasphemous? Catholics are tongue-tied and embarrassed in the face of such statements. Some begin to doubt what they have always taken for granted. Others know that the objectors are wrong, but they are at a loss as to how to answer clearly and reasonably. Enter the need for some form of apologetics. We cannot present a full-blown course in the subject here, but we will take a brief look at some of the more common issues that Catholics are confronted with.

"Why Do We Need a Church?"

The rest of the sentence usually goes something like this: "I pray to God in my own way. I live a good life. Why should I bother with some big institution with all its problems? Religion is a private matter anyway." And so forth. It seems this viewpoint is becoming increasingly common in our individualistic society.

It is an honest question for many people, and one that is difficult to answer on purely rational grounds. I would try to respond on two levels, one psychological and the other theological. On the first level I would ask the seeker to look at human experience in other important areas of life. Isn't it difficult, for example, to stick to a weight loss program all by oneself? Or an exercise program? (This is one reason why health clubs are so popular.) Millions of people recovering from addictions—alcohol, drugs, sex, gambling—will testify to the power of the support group to help them remain free. Are not the same dynamics operative in our spiritual life, our relationship with God? Do we not need the support of other faith-filled persons to pray with us, inspire us, keep us focused on spiritual realities? A purely individual relationship with God is difficult to maintain over the long haul. We are social beings by nature. For a while, perhaps, being a spiritual loner has a romantic, quasi-heroic appeal. But eventually the hunger for connection, for community kicks in, and we feel the need to belong to something larger than ourselves—what St. Paul called "the body of Christ, the Church."

On the theological level, the question has to be asked: "How does *God* want to be honored and worshiped?" The Bible gives a clear answer: Not only by individual devotion but also by belonging to a community of believers. It is true that God first made a spiritual covenant with individuals (Abraham, Isaac, Jacob), but always including "your descendants" and eventually "a host of nations" (Gn 17:5). Later, during the Exodus, God made the covenant with the entire Hebrew community, calling them to be "a kingdom of priests, a holy nation" (Ex 19:6). Finally, following Jesus' directives regarding "the church" (Mt 16:18; 18:17), the apostles and first Christians formed "a community of believers" (Acts 4:32) and identified themselves as belonging to "the church" (Acts 8:1). It follows, then, if we want to follow God's plan for our spiritual journey, we need to let go of some of our individualism and join hands and hearts with the community of God's people, the church, imperfect and unfinished as it is. It is a church, as the Second Vatican Council said, that is "holy yet always in need of renewal and reform."

Christians will generally agree with the above reflections on the need for a church community. But fundamentalist Christians often say to Catholics: "We are a Bible-believing church. The Bible alone is our rule of faith. You Catholics, on the other hand, do not know the Bible or give it full authority. Instead, you rely on your man-made doctrines and traditions put forth by your popes and bishops."

Unfortunately, it would be difficult to deny that we Catholics do not know the Bible well. We have been formed in our faith largely through our textbooks and catechisms. But that has been changing in recent years. Increasingly, the Bible has been an integral source of our religious formation. Our Sunday liturgies expose us to a rich and varied sampling of biblical texts. Former Protestant minister Scott Hahn says that the first time he attended a Catholic Mass, he was amazed at how much of the ceremony (including the eucharistic prayer) is either directly from the Bible or steeped in biblical language and themes. Moreover, nowadays the church requires that every celebration of a sacrament or even a blessing must be accompanied by readings from scripture. For years now Catholics have been encouraged to read the Bible personally and to gather in groups to study and reflect together on the sacred texts. We too are a "Bible-believing church."

On the other hand, we do not believe that the Bible stands alone as the source and norm for our faith. For one thing, nowhere in scripture do we find the expression "the Bible alone"; those are the words of Martin Luther. In fact, the Bible calls *the Church* "the pillar and foundation of truth" (1 Tm 3:15). Certainly, our beliefs must never contradict what scripture says. But, if reading the Bible is our sole source of religious truth, what do people do who can't read or don't have access to the Bible? What did Christians do who lived in the first centuries—before there was printing—and even before the Bible was finally put together? The fact is, it was not till almost four hundred years after Christ that the various books of the Bible were finally agreed upon. Before that, there were many other writings circulating among Christians which some believed to be "inspired" as scripture. Who decided? It was the church, guided by the Holy Spirit, that sifted through all these writings and finally declared: These—and only these—are the inspired Word of God. This was not achieved until the Council of Rome in the year 382 A.D. So what did Christians rely on all those years as their norm of faith? It was "Tradition"—the teachings that were handed down from the apostles and their successors. That dynamic was already at work in the first decades, as is evident from St. Paul's writings: ". . . [S]tand firm and hold fast to the traditions that you were taught, either by an oral statement or by a letter of ours" (2 Thes 2:15). And again: "And what you have heard from me through many witnesses entrust to faithful people who will have the ability to teach others as well" (2 Tm 2:2). Note the emphasis on hearing and teaching. And we know from history that when some would put forth teachings that were contrary to the witness of scripture and the tradition, the leaders would challenge them. If that did not resolve the issue, they would gather together in council and reflect: Is this teaching consistent and in continuity with what we have received from the apostles and their successors? If so, it would be incorporated into the tradition; if not, it would be condemned as heresy. This was a function of "the living church."

Another problem with "the Bible alone" approach: the scriptures are not always plain and easy to understand. They can be interpreted in various and even contradictory ways. In fact, that is exactly what has occurred frequently in history. How else can we explain the fact that presently there are more than 26,000 Christian sects in the world, all disagreeing with each other yet all claiming to follow the Bible as their rule of faith? Interestingly, the Bible itself indicates that its content is not always self-evident and needs to be explained and interpreted in the light of a living tradition. The Acts of the Apostles relates the story of a Christian evangelist named Philip and an Ethiopian official who was returning from a feast in Jerusalem. While riding in his carriage and reading the prophet Isaiah, Philip asked him, "Do you understand what you are reading?" The man replied, "How can I, unless someone instructs me?" (Acts 8:30-31). Whether the Ethiopian was a Jewish convert or a pagan "God-fearer" who was drawn to the Jewish religion, it is clear that the scripture passage was beyond his comprehension. He needed a teacher, a Spirit-guided person who was familiar with the fullness of God's revelation in Jesus Christ. I am not denying that the Holy Spirit is able to instruct and enlighten and inspire us when we read the word of God personally. But without a community, a tradition, an authority outside of ourselves, we can easily be confused or distort the true meaning of the sacred text. St. Peter alluded to this when he wrote: "In them [the letters of Paul] there are some things hard to understand that the ignorant and unstable distort to their own destruction, just as they do the other scriptures" (2 Pt 3:16).

To summarize: the Catholic Church reveres the Bible as the authentic and saving word of God. But the Bible always needs to be read and understood in light of the church's living tradition. In the early years, Christians often disagreed on the meaning of Bible texts and Christian beliefs, and even on which writings were inspired. They would look to the bishops and popes to discern and settle the issues in local and plenary councils, under the guidance of the Holy Spirit. So the Bible cannot be separated from tradition or from the teaching authority of the pope and bishops. In the early church, all three "grew up" together. (See Alan Schreck, *Catholic and Christian*, Servant Books, 1984, Ch. 2.)

"Are You Saved?"

Another issue that divides Catholics from fundamentalist Protestants is the question of salvation. What does it mean to be saved? And how does it happen? Catholics and fundamentalists can agree that salvation means being brought from a state of sin and guilt (with hell as the final consequence) to a state of forgiveness and union with God ("grace"), with heaven/eternal life as the final consequence. But the difference lies in how this transformation happens. For fundamentalists, it begins with the awareness that we are sinners, totally incapable of gaining God's favor by our own efforts. If left to ourselves, none of us could ever find forgiveness or attain heaven. But the good news is that God loved us so much that he sent his only Son to die for us on the cross, thereby atoning for our sins and making us righteous before God. However, in order to lay hold of this saving grace, each one of us must make a personal decision to repent of our sins and receive the forgiveness that God offers us in Christ. This is what it means to be "saved" or "born again" or "come to know the Lord." It is a purely internal act. No external or public ceremony (such as baptism) is required. And once I have made that act of turning to Christ as my Lord and Savior, my salvation is absolutely assured. I will not be lost. Conversely, one who has not made that personal decision cannot be saved, no matter how many prayers or "good works" they may perform through their whole life.

We can easily see, then, why fundamentalists so often regard us Catholics as among the unsaved, on the way to hell. Why? Because "you Catholics rely on your sacraments and your good works and your prayers to

Mary and the saints—and thereby deny the adequacy of Christ's death for your salvation. Furthermore, you have not made that decisive act of committing your life to Jesus Christ."

In reality, though, our differences are not that profound. We Catholics agree that we cannot save ourselves and that Jesus saved us by giving his life on the cross for love of us. We also agree that we have to take some personal responsibility for our salvation. But we do not see this as a single, once-for-all decision. It is much more a lifelong process. It begins with baptism. We take seriously Jesus' words that "no one can enter the kingdom of God without being born of water and Spirit" (Jn 3:5). Besides, baptism is a wonderful way to symbolize that, indeed, we do not save ourselves. The cleansing from sin that baptism signifies is entirely God's work. This is especially so in infant baptism, where the child has done absolutely nothing to "earn" salvation.

However, we also believe that, at some point, we need to make a personal commitment to Jesus Christ. Explicitly or implicitly, verbally or non-verbally, we say: "Lord Jesus, I don't want to live just for myself. I want you to be the center of my life. I want to avoid sin and try to please you in all that I do. I want to love you with all my heart, and my neighbor as myself, as you commanded us." As I've said earlier, perhaps too many Catholics have never made that personal decision, so they appear to be "practicing" their faith and "saying their prayers," but without much heart or sense of joy. They don't look very much like "saved" or "holy" people.

At the same time, I have met many, many Catholics who have made that commitment—and are living it. But—it is not a single, decisive act. They renew that decision over and over. Not because they don't have faith in Jesus' saving love, but simply because they are weak and forgetful. They know there are many other "voices" clamoring for their attention and many other "gods" competing for their loyalty. So they need to begin and end each day with prayer. They need to hear and read God's word in scripture. They want to receive the body and blood of their Lord in Holy Communion to be their strength. When they sin, they confess not only to God but to another weak human being whom they believe mediates God's forgiveness to them (see John 20:22-23). They believe that the sacraments are neither magic nor empty rituals. They are spiritual aids given to us by Christ himself; and all their power comes from his Cross.

As for "good works," we know they do not save us. Still, they are necessary ways to keep us growing in our relationship with Christ and being obedient to his word. That is perfectly consistent with the scriptures:

* "If you love me, you will keep my commandments" (Jn 14:15).

* "Not everyone who says to me, 'Lord, Lord', will enter the kingdom of heaven, but only the one who does the will of my Father in heaven" (Mt 7:21).

* "What good is it . . . if someone says he has faith but does not have works? Can that faith save him? . . . For just as a body without a spirit is dead, so also faith without works is dead" (Jas 2:14, 26).

As for praying to Mary and the saints, we do not ask them to help us directly. Rather, we ask them to intercede for us with God, who alone has the power to save us, heal us, and help us. Nor do we "worship" their statues and images, as is sometimes alleged. These images are no more than visual reminders, much as people's photographs of their loved ones are reminders of those who are absent physically. Finally, we believe that we can have a firm hope of salvation and of going to heaven, but not absolute assurance. For the Bible warns us often that we are fragile and always in danger of going back on our commitment. Even St. Paul did not claim absolute certainty about his salvation. Why else would he write, "Thus I do not run aimlessly; I do not fight as if I were shadowboxing. No, I drive my body and train it, for fear that, after having preached to others, I myself should be disqualified" (1 Cor 9:26-27)? It is for the same reason that he wrote to his beloved Philippians, "work out your salvation with fear and trembling" (Phil 2:12). These are sobering admonitions, not meant to frighten us but to remind us that we always stand in need of the saving grace and love of Jesus Christ. And that is also good news. (For a fuller treatment of the above issues, see my book *Catholics and Fundamentalists: Understanding the Difference*, chs. 2 and 3.)

"Why Should I Believe Church Authorities?"

This is another difficult question, especially for many people nowadays who place a high value on thinking for themselves. Again, the answer can be appreciated fully only by those who are open to belief in the supernatural and in the Bible. First, on the human level we can again appeal to human experience. Any organization or institution needs some locus of authority; without this it tends to fracture into competing subgroups and lose its cohesiveness. Even if authority resides in some sort of democratic "majority rule," that authority must be upheld if the organization is to survive. The same principle holds true for the church. If everyone was free to believe and act as he or she thinks best, the church would soon splinter into numerous factions. Has this not happened already in the Christian churches? And is this not a cause of sadness as well as scandal? This surely cannot be the will of Christ for his church.

So the question naturally arises: What sort of authority structure did Jesus desire for the church? The answer is not very explicit from the gospels, though there are a number of clear indications. First, he did gather around himself a small group of men who were named as "the Twelve" or "the apostles." Moreover, he gave them special authority to carry on his own mission: "He summoned the Twelve and gave them power and authority over all demons and to cure diseases, and he sent them to proclaim the kingdom of God and to heal [the sick]" (Lk 9:1-2). At the end of all four gospel accounts, Jesus appears to the apostles and commissions them to continue his ministry: to teach, to baptize, to make disciples of all the nations (Matthew 28:19-20). "As the Father has sent me," he says, "so I send you" (Jn 20:21), and in the next "breath" (literally) he gives them the power to forgive sins in his name (see John 20:22-23).

In themselves, these texts may or may not be read as including authority to settle disputes over the content of Jesus' teachings. But this kind of authority can be inferred from other texts. In Matthew 16:18-19 we have the famous saying of Jesus to Peter: ". . . I say to you, you are Peter, and upon this rock I will build my church, and the gates of the netherworld shall not prevail against it. I will give you the keys to the kingdom of heaven. Whatever you bind on earth shall be bound in heaven; and whatever you loose on earth shall be loosed in heaven." The Catholic Church understands this text as giving to Peter a certain primacy of teaching authority over the whole church. Later, in Matthew 18:18, the same authority (minus the reference to "the keys to the kingdom of heaven") is given by Jesus to the rest of the apostles.

The Acts of the Apostles clearly shows Peter and the other apostles acting with authority to settle doctrinal and moral disputes. The Council of Jerusalem (c. 50 A.D.) declared that Gentile converts need not obey all the prescriptions of Old Testament law (particularly circumcision) when they became Christian converts (see Acts 15). St. Paul ordered the Corinthians to excommunicate the man who was living in an incestuous relationship (1 Cor 5:1-2). Other New Testament texts make it clear that the first Christians understood that the authority to teach and to govern the church resided in leaders who were recognized as successors to the apostles. Probably the earliest New Testament writing was St. Paul's first letter to the Thessalonians, written about 50 A.D. There he says: "We ask you, brothers [and sisters], to respect those who are laboring among you and who are over you [those who exercise authority] in the Lord and who admonish you, and to show esteem for them with special love on account of their work" (1 Thes 5:12-13). Later, in the Letter to Titus we read that a bishop must be "holding fast to the true message [of the gospel] as taught so that he will be able both to exhort with sound doctrine and to refute opponents" (Ti 1:9).

As time went on and the church spread to other parts of the world, structures of organization and authority continued to develop. Each local church had its own bishop as the center of unity and authority. In the year 110 A.D., St. Ignatius, bishop of Antioch, was arrested and ordered to undergo martyrdom in Rome. On the way he wrote letters to a number of Christian churches in Asia Minor. The one to the church in Smyrna is remarkable for its testimony to the authority of local bishops:

> You should all follow the bishops as Jesus Christ did the Father. . . . Nobody must do anything that has to do with the Church without the bishop's approval. You should regard that Eucharist as valid which is celebrated either by the bishop or by someone he authorizes. Where the bishop is present, there let the congregation gather, just as where Jesus Christ is, there is the Catholic Church.

By this time, too, the bishop of Rome was recognized as the successor of Peter the apostle, and was therefore acknowledged as having supreme authority over the universal church. Before the end of the first century, the church in Rome helped to settle problems in other local churches. In 96 A.D., St. Clement, bishop of Rome, wrote a strong letter to the church in Corinth to resolve a dispute over leadership there. In 250 A.D., St. Cyprian, the bishop of Carthage in North Africa, wrote a letter "On the Unity of the Catholic Church" in which he said this about the bishop of Rome:

> It is on him (Peter) that He (Jesus) builds the church, and to him that He entrusts the sheep to feed. And although He assigns power to all the apostles, yet He founded a single chair, thus establishing by His own authority the source and hallmark of the churches' oneness. No doubt the others were all that Peter was, but a primacy is given to Peter, and it is thus made clear that there is but one church and one chair. . . . If a man does not hold fast to this oneness of Peter, does he imagine that he still holds the faith? If he deserts the Chair of Peter upon whom the church was built, has he still confidence that he is in the church?

These early Christians were not blind or naive. They knew how easily even good and sincere people can slip into ways of believing and acting that are contrary to the teachings and example of Jesus. They were also aware of the human tendency toward rivalries and jealousies, especially regarding who is "in charge." Guided by the Holy Spirit, they relied on the gifts of authority and leadership that they believed were handed down from the time of the apostles. In that way they could insure good order and continuity of faith for the whole community, now spread worldwide. Individual believers and local church communities did enjoy a great deal of freedom in their expression of faith, worship, and ministry. But finally they were subject and accountable to their pastors and bishops, so that the body of Christ might not be rent asunder by divisions. And over them all was the supreme authority of the pope, the bishop of Rome.

The above discussion reveals once again the inadequacy of "the Bible alone" theology of revelation. We will not find words like "pope" or "hierarchy" in the Bible. It requires a knowledge of early church history to understand how these structures of office and authority evolved from the general outlines presented in the scriptures. Jesus left it to the creative minds of Christians, as well as to the divine guidance of the Holy Spirit, to work out the details of teaching and governing authority for the church. These Christians shared Christ's own passion for unity among believers (Jn 17:20-21). They saw dissension and petty bickering happening in their midst, and they took steps to insure that both unity and healthy diversity would be honored. (For an excellent treatment of these issues, see Alan Schreck, *Catholic and Christian*, chs. 4 and 5.)

A final word about "papal infallibility." This is a much-misunderstood Catholic teaching. It must be stated again that infallibility has nothing to do with good judgment or with moral goodness. We have abundant evidence from history that some popes have made serious blunders of leadership and have led sinful, scandalous lives. Papal infallibility is both a very narrow and a very necessary concept. It claims that the pope cannot teach substantive error when he speaks *ex cathedra*—that is, when he speaks as supreme teacher of the universal church in a matter of Christian belief or morality. This has been an extremely rare occurrence in the history of the church. Popes do not wake up in the morning thinking about what they will declare to be infallible today. It is only when a serious matter of faith or morals is being questioned or raised anew that a pope might invoke his supreme teaching authority. And he is not qualified, for example, to judge the literary merits of a book or to settle a disputed point in biochemistry. Still, the doctrine is necessary in order to safeguard the content of divine revelation. For if the pope could fall into substantive error in his teaching, the faithful would never be sure what to believe. In that sense, infallibility is a gift of the Holy Spirit for the spiritual good of the whole church, not for the personal glory of the pope.

One final point. While the church's teaching authority is indeed a gift, it can also be abused. In too many instances, both past and present, the church has used its authority to stifle creative thinking and development of new forms of worship and ministry. This has been tragic, not only for the suffering it has caused for the innovators, but for the whole church. Certainly, we must respect the right of the church to correct error and to maintain good order. But there is no excuse for harassment of scholars who are exploring new ways to understand some teaching, no excuse for publicly scolding bishops who allow practices that may be against the letter of the law but are well within its spirit. These kinds of actions only provoke discouragement in believers, plus scorn and ridicule in the church's critics. They surely do not advance the cause of evangelization. I pray for the day when church authorities will develop more human and Christian ways to deal with those who dissent or push the limits of acceptable teaching.

"The Real Presence"

The last "objection" we will consider in this chapter on apologetics has to do with the Sacrament of the Eucharist. Historically, Catholics have maintained that the eucharist, contains the real presence of Christ— "body, blood, soul, and divinity" is the standard formula—while for Protestants, it is only a sign or symbol of that presence. Catholics sometimes note, with a certain irony, that fundamentalist Christians tend to understand the Bible's words literally—except when it comes to the eucharist; then they slip into a symbolic interpretation. We will look at the scriptures first.

A good starting point would be the sixth chapter of John's gospel. It begins with the multiplication of the loaves and fishes. But then Jesus tells the crowd that God wants to give them "bread from heaven." When they express a desire for it, he tells them that he himself is "the bread of life," the true bread from heaven in whom they are to believe. Thus far he has been talking about the necessity of putting their faith in him rather than in anything earthly. But then he startles them by saying, "the bread that I will give is my flesh for the life of the world" (6:51). Taking his words literally, they object: "How can this man give us his flesh to eat?" At this point readers of John's gospel would expect Jesus to correct them for misunderstanding him, as he has so often done before (see Jn 2:19-21; 3:4-8; 4:7-15; 4:32-34). Instead, he insists on a more literal meaning: "Amen, amen, I say to you, unless you eat the flesh of the Son of Man and drink his blood, you do not have life within you. . . . For my flesh is true food and my blood is true drink. Whoever eats my flesh and drinks my blood remains in me and I in him" (Jn 6:53, 55-56). And at that point even some of his own disciples are turned off: "This saying is hard; who can accept it?" (vs. 60). Many of them even walked away and no longer followed him (vs. 66). But again, Jesus did not back down or give a symbolic interpretation. Instead, he turned to the Twelve and said, "Do you also want to leave?" (vs. 67). And Peter reassured him that they had nowhere else to go: "You have the words of eternal life. We have come to believe and are convinced that you are the Holy One of God" (vv. 68-69). Peter and the others obviously did not grasp the full meaning of Jesus' words, but they trusted him enough to want to stay in his company.

This passage is often called "the promise of the eucharist." The fulfillment, we Catholics believe, took place at the Last Supper. All three synoptic gospels record Jesus speaking the same words over the loaf of bread and the cup of wine: "This is my body. . . . This is my blood" (Mt 26:26-28; Mk 14:22-24; Lk 22:17-20). In an even earlier writing, St. Paul tells the Corinthians that he has "received from the Lord what I also handed on to you"; and he goes on to describe the Last Supper scene, using the same words: This IS my body; this IS my blood (see 1 Corinthians 11:23-26). And as if to emphasize the truth of Christ's real presence, Paul goes on to say: "Therefore whoever eats the bread or drinks the cup of the Lord unworthily will have to answer for the body and blood of the Lord" (vs. 27). How could he say that if the eucharist were merely a symbol?

And again, we have historical evidence that the early Christians believed that the Eucharist was the sacrament of the real rather than the symbolic presence of Christ. St. Justin Martyr, around 150 A.D., wrote in his "apology" to the (pagan) emperor of Rome:

> We call this food Eucharist; and no one else is permitted to partake of it, except one who believes our teaching to be true. . . . For not as common bread nor common drink do we receive these; but since Jesus Christ our Savior was made incarnate by the word of God and had both flesh and blood for our salvation, so too, as we have been taught, the food which has been made into the Eucharist by the Eucharistic Prayer set down by Him, and by the change of which our blood and flesh is nourished, is both the Flesh and the Blood of that incarnated Jesus.

Two centuries later, St. Cyril of Jerusalem said in one of his catechetical lectures: "Do not, therefore, regard the bread and wine as simply that; for they are, according to the Master's declaration, the Body and Blood of Christ. Even though the senses suggest to you the other, let faith make you firm. Do not judge in this matter by taste, but be fully assured by the faith, not doubting that you have been deemed worthy of the Body and Blood of Christ." Interestingly, even Martin Luther affirmed the doctrine of the real presence:

> Who ever read in the Scriptures that *my body* is the same as *the sign of my body*? Or that *it is* the same as *it signifies*? What language in the world ever spoke so? . . . Not one of the Fathers [of the Church], though so numerous . . . ever said, 'It is only bread and wine;' or 'the body and blood of Christ is not there present.' . . . Certainly in so many Fathers, and in so many writings, the negative might be found in at least one of them, had they thought the body and blood of Christ were not really present; but they are all of them unanimous. (*Luther's Collected Works*, Wittenburg Edition, n. 7, p. 391)

Conclusion

I want to emphasize that apologetics is a relatively minor part of evangelization. Here as elsewhere, a little knowledge can be dangerous. Armed with a few Bible texts and a few quotes from early church authorities, overzealous Catholics can end up "picking fights" with other Christians and get caught up in fruitless arguments that only serve to alienate the very people they are trying to win over. As I said earlier, evangelization always begins with living our faith, giving an example of Christian love, moral integrity, and a spirit of joy. It involves listening and encouraging others to share their human struggles and their spiritual longings. Usually, the most effective way of evangelizing is not by engaging in apologetics but by simply sharing one's own experience of faith, of discovering God's presence and help in one's daily life. Still, some knowledge of apologetics can be very helpful when seekers ask questions about our beliefs, or when they raise objections. And even if the evangelizer does not know how to answer on the spot, he or she can offer to find out and get back to the seeker. In any case, we always need to follow the exhortation of St. Peter to speak "with gentleness and reverence" (1 Pt 3:16). (A list of resources for apologetics can be found at the end of this book.)

Some Final Comments

I began this book by asking, "Where is the passion?" Or, in the words of Pope Paul VI in the beginning of his apostolic exhortation on evangelization, "In our day, what has happened to that hidden energy of the Good News. . . ?" My hope in writing this book is that it will reawaken "the hidden energy" slumbering in many of our people, the passion to make Jesus Christ and his gospel known and loved in every way possible.

My own "conversion" to evangelization has been a long one. My first assignment after ordination was to study for a doctorate in counseling psychology. After obtaining the degree I spent about fifteen years counseling priests, religious, and laity, and teaching pastoral counseling courses in a seminary. I had no familiarity with the concept of evangelization. I believe it was in 1976 that I either heard or read a talk by Paulist Fr. Alvin Illig on evangelization. I remember being deeply moved as he spoke of the need for the church to reach out to the vast numbers of people who are not being reached by our ordinary parish ministries. He quoted frequently from Pope Paul VI's document *On Evangelization in the Modern World*, a text I hadn't even heard of. I soon got my hands on it, and again it was an eye-opener as well as a heart-mover. I felt a call to do something by way of evangelization. But a few months later my Order asked me to take on the job of directing our novitiate program, so I was unable to do much else besides keep reading and educating myself. I did help two of our friars begin a small evangelizing ministry in connection with the novitiate.

Seven years later I began working in one of our retreat centers. My third year there we based our retreat on the theme of evangelization. We were surprised and pleased to see how enthused the laity became about the topic, once they understood it. The next year I was asked to return to seminary teaching. I agreed, but on the condition that I would be able also to teach a course on evangelization. The seminary agreed, and opened the course to include laity. By this time I had developed, besides the academic course, a brief (four session) training course on how to evangelize one-to-one, and I began to offer it both at the seminary and in parishes. A few years later I left full time teaching to establish a store front evangelization center in Racine, Wisconsin. Later, when I was transferred to Detroit, I realized the importance of training laity to conduct the training course; this has multiplied the number of people we are able to reach. Later still I moved back to Milwaukee, where I worked with the archdiocese to help parishes begin or further develop their evangelizing ministry. Now that I am again in retreat work, I am working in a similar way with parishes in the Diocese of La Crosse, Wisconsin. Again, what I am finding is that there is a strong desire among our Catholic people to understand evangelization and how to actually carry it out, both individually and as parishes. I have long wanted to write a book like this, but I felt I was not ready until I had more experience. Now is the time.

In conclusion, I wish to stress again the need for greater passion in our ministry. As Fr. John Cusick put it so well in that interview I noted earlier: "What we need, and what many in church ministry no longer have, is missionary zeal. Are we in fact in love with our people?" I believe we are. But perhaps we are reluctant to challenge them. Yes, we are busy—and so are they.

Yet, is there anything more exciting, anything more worthy of our time and energy, than making known the good news of Jesus Christ?

Let me close with the stirring words of Pope John Paul II to representatives of the whole Franciscan Family gathered in Rome in 1982—words that apply to every one of us: "Go, you who are the friars [brothers] of the people, into the heart of the masses, to those teeming multitudes, wandering aimlessly and dejected like sheep without a shepherd, those very ones for whom Christ felt compassion. . . . Go you also to the men and women of our time. Don't wait for them to come to you! You yourselves must seek them out. It is love which drives you to do this. . . . The whole Church will be grateful to you."

APPENDIX

Sample Letter to All on Parish Membership List

Dear Brother/Sister in Christ:

For some time now our parish has been concerned about the people who are not being reached by our ordinary parish services. We are aware, for example, that there are many baptized Catholics who feel left out of parish life for whatever reason. We do not want to be indifferent to them. We want them to know that we miss them and to know that they are welcome in our parish family. So we have designed a ministry that we are calling "Welcome Home." We are now ready to begin, and we are asking your support.

If you are an active member of our parish, we ask two things of you. First, that you **pray** earnestly and regularly for God's blessing on this outreach. We want God's grace to touch the hearts of people who are seeking for spiritual meaning in their lives.

Second, we ask you to personally talk with people (family members, friends, co-workers, etc.) who are Catholic by baptism but are not presently practicing their faith, for whatever reason. We do not want you to pressure them or argue with them. Simply **invite** them to what we are calling a "Listening Session" (date and time will be announced). This will be an opportunity for them to tell us about their difficulties with the church and how we might help them. There will be no fee, no obligation to rejoin. We simply want to meet them and listen to them. The "listening team" will consist of our pastor and a small group of parishioners who have been trained for this ministry.

You may feel a bit awkward about doing this, but we ask you to pray for guidance and then to try it. Research has shown that there are a lot of inactive Catholics who would like to reconnect with the church but don't know how, or are not sure they would be welcome. But they would be grateful if someone would reach out to them first. In any case, what do you have to lose? All they can do is say no.

Finally, if you are an inactive Catholic yourself, we want to extend a special invitation to you to attend the Listening Session. We miss you. Perhaps you feel disappointed in the church or in our parish, and we want to understand why. Or, you may have been hurt by someone in the church, and we want to Papologize for that. In any case, we would invite you to come and take "another look" at who we are today as the Body of Christ.

Sample Letter for Neighborhood Visitation

Dear Neighbor,

The church(es) of our neighborhood are planning a door-to-door visit in the coming weeks. We believe it is the purpose and mission of the local church to serve not only its own members but also to be of service to everyone in the neighborhood. We are looking forward to meeting with you and talking with you about your spiritual needs and other concerns you may have, including the neighborhood itself.

If you are already a member of our church community, we hope you will share with us your ideas about how we can improve our services, and how you might be willing to share your talents and abilities to further our mission.

[If the letter is being sent only from a Catholic parish:] If you are a baptized Catholic but no longer attending church, we want to understand why or how the church may have hurt or disappointed you. We do miss you, and we would like to invite you, without any pressure, to take "another look" at who we are today. If you are an active member of another religion or denomination, we will not ask you to change. We will simply ask you to pray for us as we attempt to reach out in the name of God.

And finally, you may be among the eighty million Americans with no church affiliation. But perhaps you are searching for a deeper meaning in life, for some kind of spiritual grounding, perhaps for a sense of belonging to a caring community. If so, we want to invite you, again without pressure, to at least consider connecting with us or with some other faith community.

We trust you will receive our visit in the same spirit in which we make it. We look forward to meeting you and ask your prayers for God's blessing on our efforts.

Your Brothers and Sisters at. . . .

Resources for Evangelization

General

Archdiocese of Milwaukee. *Evangelization Handbook for Parishes* (printed 1998). A set of articles and resources for parish use. The archdiocese also has available a wall chart of how evangelization can be integrated into existing parish structures and ministries.

Bausch, William. *The Hands-On Parish* (Twenty-Third Publications, 1989). Not much on evangelization itself, but many good ideas on how to involve parishioners in ongoing renewal.

Bausch, William. *While You Were Gone: A Handbook for Returning Catholics* (Twenty-Third Publications, 1994). A gentle approach to help inactive Catholics who are returning to the church (or thinking about it) to deal with the changes they will encounter, while assuring them that the essence of Catholic faith has remained constant.

Boyack, Kenneth, CSP (ed.). *The New Catholic Evangelization* (Paulist, 1992). A collection of readings by a fine group of authors dedicated to furthering the message of the gospel in contemporary culture. Each chapter concludes with a set of discussion questions.

Brennan, Patrick. *The Evangelizing Parish* (Tabor, 1987). A valuable collection of suggestions for ways of rethinking parish organization and for developing pastoral attitudes toward inactive Catholics.

Brennan, Patrick. *The Reconciling Parish* (Tabor, 1990). A fine follow-up to his previous book, with emphasis on helping the parish to become a welcoming and reconciling community.

Brennan, Patrick. *Re-Imagining Evangelization* (Crossroad, 1995). Building on his previous works plus his experience as a pastor, Brennan develops the concept of "the communal parish" where everyone is called to ministry and to participation in small faith communities.

Celek, Tim and Dieter Zander. *Inside the Soul of a New Generation* (Zondervan, 1996). Written by two evangelical pastors in popular style, the book is an insightful analysis of "Generation X" along with helpful suggestions on how to reach them with the gospel.

Champlin, Joseph. *The Marginal Catholic* (Ave Maria Press, 1989). A compassionate guide for parish ministers who are approached by non-practicing Catholics seeking baptism for their children or marriage for themselves.

DeSiano, Frank and Kenneth Boyack. *Creating the Evangelizing Parish* (Paulist, 1993). Authors present "an encounter model" of evangelization based on personal relations. Filled with practical strategies for parish-based evangelization.

DeSiano, Frank and Kenneth Boyack. *Discovering My Experience of God* (Paulist, 1992). A brief but fine explanation of the role of personal religious experience for our own growth in faith and for evangelizing others. Includes a practical workbook for helping readers get in touch with their experience.

Hater, Robert. *News That Is Good* (Ave Maria Press, 1990). Subtitled "Evangelization for Catholics," this is a great introduction to evangelization, with a lot of practical examples. Not much on parish programs, though.

Kemp, C. and D. Pologruto. *Catholics Coming Home* (Harper/San Francisco, 1990). A step-by-step description of a parish-based program for reaching out and reconciling inactive Catholics.

Mews, Sally L. *Catholics Returning Home* (privately printed). A six-session program of outreach and reconciliation of inactive Catholics. Manual gives step-by-step process for use by parishes. Contact Sally Mews at 847-855-0629.

Pable, Martin, OFM Cap. and Sandra McConnell, SFO. *Empowerment to Personal Evangelization* (privately printed, 2000). Manual for a training course for Catholics on how to share their faith one-to-one in ordinary situations. Contact Sandra McConnell at 248-651-4826.

Smith, Donald P. *How to Attract and Keep Active Church Members* (Westminister/Knox, 1992). Acknowledging the fact that membership dropout is a serious problem, this Presbyterian pastor examines causes and makes positive suggestions for addressing the felt needs of church members.

Strobel, Lee. *Inside the Mind of Unchurched Harry and Mary* (Zondervan, 1993). Written by a formerly secularized and unchurched person himself, Strobel gives a penetrating analysis of the typical secular American and how the churches can succeed in reaching them.

Sullivan, Joseph T. *How to Share Your Faith With Others* (Liguori, 2000). Written by a diocesan priest, the book gives practical suggestions on how to dialogue one-to-one with seekers. Question-and-answer format inclines toward superficiality.

Apologetics

U.S. Catholic Conference. *Catechism of the Catholic Church* (Washington, D.C., 1994).

Chacon, Frank and Jim Burnham. *Beginning Apologetics* (San Juan Catholic Seminars, 1993-99). A series of six booklets by a priest and a layman, covering a variety of topics including dealing with Mormons and Jehovah's Witnesses.

Currie, David. *Born Fundamentalist, Born Again Catholic* (Ignatius Press, 1996). One man's story of his conversion to Catholicism, with intelligent discussions of key doctrinal issues.

Hahn, Scott and Kimberly. *Rome Sweet Home* (Ignatius Press, 1993). Story of Protestant minister and wife's spiritual journey and conversion. The Hahns have also produced many tapes on apologetic questions.

Kreeft, Peter. *Fundamentals of the Faith* (Ignatius Press, 1988). Subtitled "Essays in Christian Apologetics," the author deals with basic questions like the existence of God, the divinity of Christ, and comparative religions, as well as common objections to Catholic beliefs.

LeBar, James L. *Cults, Sects, and the New Age* (Our Sunday Visitor, 1989). Several priest-authors teamed up on this work, which includes a discussion of Satanism.

Madrid, Patrick. *Surprised by Truth* (Basilica Press, 1994). Eleven people share their biblical and historical reasons for becoming Catholic. However, it includes only one woman's story.

O'Malley, William, S.J. *Why Be Catholic?* (Crossroad, 1994). A popular but solidly intelligent presentation of Catholic teaching from one of the fine writers of our time.

Pable, Martin, OFM Cap. *Catholics and Fundamentalists: Understanding the Difference* (HI-TIME and ACTA, 1997).

This updated edition explains the origin and appeal of fundamentalism, and gives clear presentations of misunderstood Catholic teachings. Also available in Spanish: *Catolicos Y Fundamentalistas.*

Schreck, Alan. *Catholic and Christian* (Servant Books, 1984). Solid, biblically-grounded discussions of Catholic teachings that are often challenged by evangelical Protestants.

MARTIN W. PABLE, OFM CAP., has spent his career in service to the church and his Capuchin community as a college and seminary professor, novitiate director, and author. He is the author of four books, including *The Quest for the Male Soul* (Ave Maria Press), and numerous articles. Presently he is retreat director at St. Anthony Retreat Center in Marathon, Wisconsin.